The Power of RE

Recreate Your Life from the Inside-Out

———————

Gary Gzik

The Power of RE
Copyright © 2010 by BizXcel Inc.

All rights reserved. No part of this book may be reproduced or transmitted in any form or by any means without written permission from the author.

ISBN 978-0-9864850-2-2

Printed in the USA.

DEDICATION

This book is dedicated to Molly, Lilly, Sam, Dallas and Molly (yes, there are two). For your unconditional love and support, your energy and playful nature, and, of course, the countless hours you have lain at our feet. You truly are our best friends.

To every dog on this Earth, we can all learn from your capacity to love and your endless curiosity to explore every opportunity life brings your way.

> "My little dog - a heartbeat at my feet."
> - Edith Wharton

ACKNOWLEDGEMENTS

Two books within six months of each other! Where do I begin to express my thanks and gratitude?

I receive inspiration every day from so many special people in my life, personally and professionally, and for this I thank each and every one of you. You are all an extraordinary gift in my life.

To my work family, your insanity keeps me sane. Your creativity is contagious and your support is overwhelming. I smile every morning thinking of the high jinxes we will get into each day. You all played your own unique role in creating these pages and I thank you.

Renée, you are a shining star. Your gift for words, tireless work without seeking recognition and your subtle cracking of the whip were instrumental to the success of this book.

To my family, Mom and Dad, you laid the foundation with principles, love and support. Jane, Evan and Hannah, you kept the flame of my inspiration burning bright.

And lastly, to the conductor of this great orchestration we call life, God. You create new opportunities every day for me to choose a purposeful life.

CONTENTS

Introduction 1
1. REgain Your Balance 11
2. REbuild Your Resilience 35
3. REimagine Your Life 71
4. REclaim Control 93
5. REnew Your Confidence 119
6. REenergize Yourself 147
7. REinvest in You 163
8. REalize the Moment 187
Conclusion 205

PREFACE

An anonymous person once said, "My goal in life is to be as good of a person as my dog already thinks I am." Isn't this the truth? Who else sees you as being perfect, loving and wonderful? Only two: Your children and your dog. In their eyes you can do no wrong. You are an all powerful superhero who has it all together.

What if you could view yourself the same way your kids and dog see you? How would your life be different if each day you believed that you could accomplish anything you set your mind to?

Over the years, I have put great effort into building the person I want to be. Each day, I assess the image I see reflected back at me to see if it matches the one I'm striving for. It has taken time and dedication, but every day I come a little bit closer to attaining my goal.

As a coach, I've watched many people struggle with this same challenge, and I've seen many of them fail. Defeat and surrender have come in many different forms: tough times wore them down, they didn't believe in themselves, they lost control of life or they didn't take the time to recharge and invest in themselves. They forgot to slow down and appreciate the fullness that life has to offer.

This is why I decided to write this book. I want you to know that inside you is the superhero your kids and dog see. You are endowed with the power of RE. While it may not seem like much, it has the ability to transform you and your whole life, like Clark Kent into Superman. You may not be able to leap over tall buildings or stop a speeding bullet, but you can leap out and grab the opportunities that come your way and stop to appreciate all the good things in your life.

The Power of RE is about taking control of your life and the person you want to be. It is about bringing more joy and happiness into your days. So find a comfortable seat, call Fido up onto your lap and enjoy.

INTRODUCTION

I wrote this book because I want to save dogs. That's right, dogs. I think people are great, but there's nothing more loyal than a dog that will stay by your side, even when you're at your worst. There's an old joke that says put your wife and your dog in the trunk of a car for an hour and see who's still happy to see you when you unlock it.

I have two wonderful dogs, Molly, a rag tagged Shih Tzu, and Lilly, our chubby Miniature Daschund. While both of them are getting on in age now – Molly needs help to get up and down the stairs and Lilly toddles more than runs – I know they will both be waiting faithfully for me at the door when I come home each night, happiness filling their big brown eyes at the sight of me. This is more than I can say most times about my teenagers.

So, you might be wondering what this book has to do with dogs. Well, as I discussed in my last book, *The Orange Popsicle*, many of us are having trouble living lives that leave us feeling happy and fulfilled. One of the reasons for this is we are unhappy with ourselves and feel we can and should be so much more than we are. Each of us carries a potential to be something great, but for many this is never realized.

When you are discontented with who you are inside, this disrupts your life. When you aren't happy, the people around you pick up on this and it rubs off on them. Think of it this way, you wake up each morning and go into a job you don't like. You know you want something more, but don't think you have the skills and ability to go after the job you really want. You worry about quitting and not being able to find another job to support your family, but you're becoming burned out by all the long hours you work and your family is upset that they don't get to spend time with you.

One morning, as you sit staring at your screen at work, your boss comes into your office and lays into you about an issue with a project that wasn't your fault. All day you stew about this injustice and how unfair it is.

That night when you go home, your spouse says something that rubs you the wrong way so you get upset with her. Now she's in a bad mood. She notices your son's sneakers left in the hallway and yells at him to put them away. Your son now angry about the trouble he's in stomps upstairs and shouts at his little sister for being in his room. As your sweet baby girl leaves the room in tears she sees the ever faithful, loving family dog quietly sleeping in the hallway and with the tiny foot he licked just that morning making her giggle hysterically, she kicks him, saying "stupid dog."

Do you see the chain affect that your unhappiness with yourself can have on those around you? Do you see the poor innocent victim that is the dog? Happiness with one's life requires a sense of happiness with one's self. You can't be contented with your life if you aren't content with who you are and how you feel.

Throughout your life there will come points when you need to reassess the direction you are going. This comes back to the concept of "someday." For a lot of people, their somedays revolve around this notion of creating a happier self: "Someday I'll take time for me," "Someday I'll have the confidence to ask for a raise," "Someday I'll spend more time at home than the office."

Your overall happiness is dependent on you believing you are the best you can be and working towards that. You can not feel happy about your life if you are not happy with yourself. I like to explain happiness through the Happiness Quotient Continuum (HQC). This shows you how you reach happiness over time. Don't be mistaken in thinking happiness is a quick fix. True happiness takes time and dedication. It's an active effort that involves changing all aspects of your lifestyle in order to achieve more fulfillment out of life.

It is necessary for you to make your somedays a reality by creating a stable path towards them on your

HQC. You need to set your sights on what makes you happy and then create the right frame of mind, practice the right habits daily and behave in a consistent way in order to set the foundation for a more enjoyable and fulfilling life.

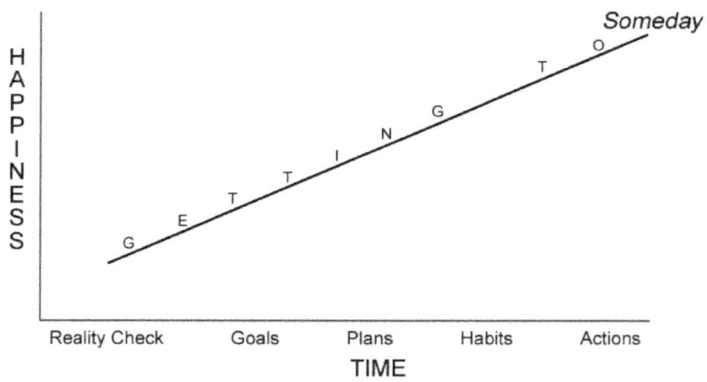

Unfortunately, instead of following a stable path in their HQC to reach these somedays, taking the proper steps to set and achieve goals to improve themselves, some people fall prey to gratification bounces when they need immediate enjoyment. These make them feel good about themselves for a while, giving them a spike of happiness, but this is then followed by a crash. These happiness fixes could be drinking too much after a bad day at work, putting down a friend to make yourself feel superior or lying about your qualifications to get a better job.

Instead of working steadily to reach your goals, you stray from the path in order to get a fix which then creates a spike in your graph. The problem with this spike is it is usually short lived and leads to the inevitable crash.

Quick and easy, these fixes are hard to pass by. There will be times when you think you must have them in order to feel good about yourself; resist. You may start to confuse them with true happiness instead of working towards your goals of building a better you and working towards happiness over time. These fixes are based on decisions that do not support the HQC, they may even be immoral, unethical or even illegal.

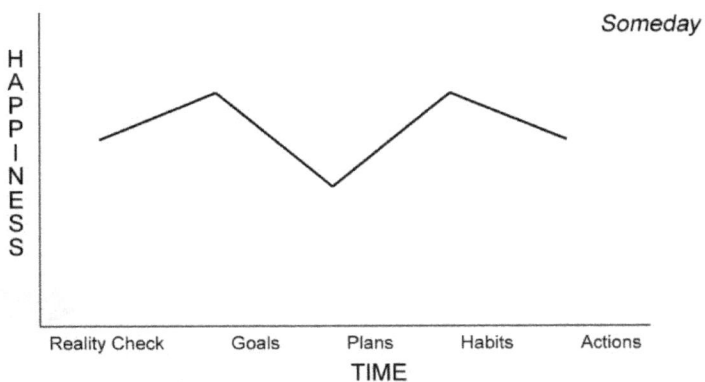

Let's look at the inverse of the HQC. Since habits create our experiences and ultimately our end results. If you are not happy and have not been happy for a while, does it not make sense that your unhappiness is an accumulation of the choices and habits you've made? Just like the HQC, where your happiness grows over time by identifying your someday and aligning your habits and actions, your unhappiness or misery develops over time due to the misalignment of your actions or just having bad habits.

When you don't take control of your life, or lack reality checks, goals, plans, habits and actions, then you quickly become a victim of circumstance and your environment. This can facilitate a downward slide to a joyless life. But you have the choice to change all this.

Happiness Downward Slide

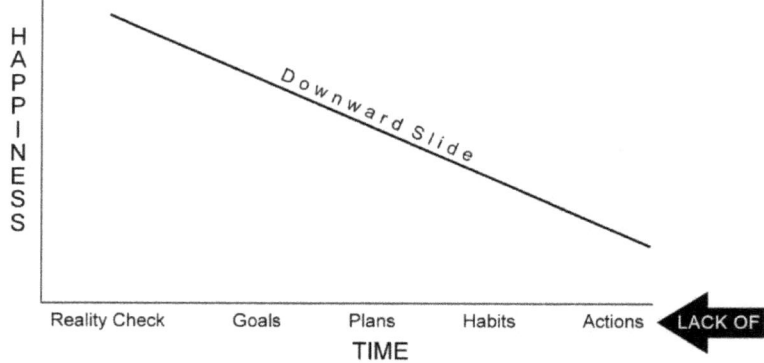

The Power of RE is based upon the premise that we all need to take time throughout our lives when we are run down and unhappy to reenergize, revitalize and recreate ourselves from the inside out. Embrace it and take yourself to the next stage of your life journey. Change is a natural part of life, but many people shy away from it to their own detriment. They are afraid to take the next step to move forward in their HQC. Mignon McLaughlin said, "It's the most unhappy people who fear change." Like all things we must change in order to grow. If you remain stagnant and refuse to alter or modify, you will live as a lesser version of your true self in a life of half-happiness.

It is odd that many people look at change with trepidation. The process of renewal surrounds us all the time. Plants grow and flourish, bloom and wither. They lay dormant under the soil during harsh winter only to poke through the ground each spring with new abundance. Trees can be cut down, yet in due time sprouts will appear around the stump. These will go on to produce leaves, branches and flowers. Eventually, a new tree will form out of the old.

Our own bodies on a microscopic level are constantly replenishing and revitalizing. The cells that line our stomach renew daily and muscle cells will regenerate after significant injury. When our cells have exceeded their lifespan or are not functioning usefully, they are programmed to die. Some will even die in order to allow the progression of growth – vast amounts kick the bucket to create neural connections in an infant's brain.

While this is normal and natural to us, we often forget about our bodies amazing capabilities to restore itself. Even if we are aware of it on a subconscious level, many of us fail to understand our ability to apply this to our lives on a conscious level.

We fall out of balance and allow ourselves to get worn down and tired. We lose control and our confidence falters. We forget just how unique and wonderful we can be. We forget that at any moment we can choose to change our lives. We fear the possible repercussions of being something different. However, it is through change and renewal that we find our true identity. Lynn Hall said, "We do not change as we grow older; we just become more clearly ourselves." And from this we derive happiness because we are comfortable with who we are. Happiness is the by-product.

You don't need permission from anyone else to take the leap, only yourself. Let this book be your permission to you to start changing, to find the real you. Use your power of RE to become the person waiting to break free inside of you.

And remember, you are taking part in a noble deed. You are saving dogs.

*"We come into this world head first and go out feet first;
in between, it is all a matter of balance."*
- Paul Boese

CHAPTER ONE: REgain Your Balance

Here's the plain and simple truth: You cannot do it all, experience it all, be it all and still remain balanced and happy. We all want to get ahead in life. It's human nature. The feeling we get from being able to provide for ourselves and our families, to afford a new house or buy a new car, to help an aging parent or simply just do the best job we can, is immeasurable.

There's nothing wrong with wanting these things. The challenge comes when we continually strive to accomplish them all and forget to take time to benefit from the accomplishments. As the old saying goes, there's not much point in earning a living if you can't live the living you're earning. This is when people fall into the "someday honeys." You may have caught yourself saying, "Someday, honey, we'll go on a vacation" or "Someday, honey, I'll take up that hobby" or "Someday, honey, I'm going to be able to spend more time with you and the family." These happen because you become so busy focusing on finding happiness through accomplishment alone that you sometimes forget to take the time to enjoy what you already have right in front of you on a daily basis.

Are you physically and emotionally drained at the end of the day? Do you never seem to get to the end of your to-do lists at work or home? Is one part of your life taking over the rest? Are you finding it hard to spend time with your friends or family? If you answered "yes" to these, you are most likely struggling with balance in your own life. In order to regain balance you need to start focusing on the things that matter the most to you.

The other day I was down at the beach not far from my house with my wife, Jane. I was watching the kids play in the water wondering where time went with my own kids. One industrious little guy caught my attention. He was playing amongst the waves, with a look of intense concentration you only ever see on the faces of small children, his brow furrowed and tongue poking out the side of his mouth. He was using a little plastic shovel to fill a yellow bucket with water, sand, shells and rocks. Back and forth he'd trudge through the waves, hauling this bucket from the water to the beach.

Watching him, it made me remember a story I'd heard a while ago about a teacher trying to teach his students the importance of evaluating the things in life in order to balance them all correctly. He brought a large empty jar and he proceeded to fill it with rocks, not unlike the little boy. He asked the students if the jar was full.

They unanimously agreed that it was. He then picked up a handful of pebbles and poured these into the jar. He shook it lightly and the pebbles rolled into the open areas between the rocks. He asked the students if the jar was full and they all agreed again that it was. Then the teacher picked up a box of sand and poured it into the jar. The sand filled up everything else. "Now," the teacher said, "I want you to recognize this as your life." The rocks are the important things: your kids, your spouse, your family, your health and your friends. If you had nothing else, your life would still be full. The pebbles are the other things that matter, like your job, your house and your car. The sand is everything else. If you put the sand into the jar first, there's no room for the pebbles or the rocks. If you put the pebbles in before the rocks, the rocks won't fit. The same goes for your life. If you spend all our time and energy on the small things, you'll never have room for the important items in your life."

What are the rocks in your life? Are you making sure you put them in your jar or bucket first?

It's a challenge trying to balance the important factors in life with the necessary things while still finding time for you. What makes it even more taxing is that life has a way of coming along and pushing you now and then causing you to have to rework your balance. Don't ever think that once you achieve a good balance that there is nothing left to do; personal balance is something that always needs adjusting. It takes constant care and vigilance along with an acceptance that change is a necessary component of balance. Albert Einstein said, "Life is like a bicycle. To keep your balance you must keep moving."

Imagine yourself standing on a high wire. The wind is ruffling your hair, birds are flying by. When you look down, you're startled to see that you are precariously perched above a deep cavern filled with rushing rapids far below. Unnerved, and starting to sweat now, you look across to the other side where your goals, aspirations and dreams are. The wire is your life. In order to make the journey to the other side you must maintain your balance, poise and a sense of security. If you are overloaded at work, your relationship with your spouse will suffer, thus you will find yourself flailing your arms in order to remain on the wire. If you are overwhelmed with helping a sick parent you may sway and one of your feet may lose its grip. No one can survive in this type of heart pounding environment for long. On the other hand, you cannot remain unmoving for fear of falling. You must go forward. Stand still too long and life will pass you by. Life isn't easy, but you must trust yourself to be able to find your own balance to succeed or you will never reach your goals.

Karl Wallenda, patriarch of the world famous "the Great Wallendas," once told the story of how he became a tightrope walker to a reporter. As a boy in Germany, he answered an ad asking for someone who could do a handstand. Simple enough, he knew he could do a handstand. However, it was what the ad didn't say that changed everything. Louis Weitzman, the prospective employer and circus performer, took the boy up a ladder to a platform 40 feet in the air. Taking a few steps across the high wire, young Karl in tow, he said, "Just walk behind me and when I bend a little, you get up and do a handstand on my shoulders." Looking down at the ground below, Karl shook his head and said he couldn't do it. "You do it," said Weitzman, "or I'll shake you off the wire." Karl did do it and he went on to be one of the most memorable high wire acts in the world before falling to his death in 1978.

Sometimes we all need this push to get going. We need someone to shake the wire to get us moving so we can learn what it takes to keep our balance and move across the beam. Karl Wallenda did not believe in safety nets. He once told an interviewer that "Gott [God] give us the courage and gift of talent to do our acts and when he be ready to take us, he will." There are no safety nets in life either, but you also have courage and your own special talent to take you across the cavern.

Balance is imperative to your sense of control and confidence, as well as how much happiness and success you have in life. You cannot spend all your energy just hanging in there. When people are out of balance, they feel overwhelmed, out of control, guilty and inadequate. They experience disruptions in their sleep, such as insomnia, increases in bad habits, like smoking and drinking, can be extremely irritable, prone to quick mood swings, anxiety and depression. Are you experiencing any of these? Do you have the need to do everything, be everywhere and solve everyone's problems? If so, it's time for you to start incorporating ways to balance yourself. Jessye Norman, the famous opera singer, said that problems arise when you have to find a balance between what people need from you and what you need from yourself. Many of us struggle with allowing our own needs to take precedence over those close to us.

The one area that people wrestle with the most is balancing their work life with their home life. Because we derive so much of our "self" from what is on our business card or what supplies that pay cheque at the end of the week that allows us to put food in our kids' mouths and clothes on their backs, it can be hard to break away. Furthermore, work often feeds our need for accomplishment. As humans, we love completion. Many people take great pride in being able to say they did or created something great.

It is easy to get caught up in society's definition of success. Are you consciously accomplishing what you want or are you just accomplishing things you feel you should? The dog wags the tail, not the other way around.

Life isn't about just work. Your life shouldn't follow the motto Live to Work. Remember the movie *Click* where Adam Sandler plays Michael Newman, an overworked, underpaid architect that gets no respect from his boss? He reaches the end of his rope when he has to cancel the family's Fourth of July camping trip because he needs to finish a project on time. At this point, Morty (who we later find out is an Angel of Death, sorry for the spoiler) provides him with the answer he's searching for in the form of a universal remote. No ordinary remote, this one allows him to control his life, fast forwarding and rewinding at will. Relieved to finally have a way out, Michael fast forwards to his promotion not realizing that means he misses out on a whole year of his life. Devastated, he decides to not use the remote again.

However, complications arise when the remote starts to overrule his choices based on his "preferences," which in the past were giving priority to his work and neglecting family issues. Michael learns the hard lesson about what you miss out on when you put one aspect of your life ahead of others. In one heart wrenching scene Michael finds out his dog has died when he's been in fast forward mode. Remember, we're saving the dogs, people!

Work should be something that enhances, not detracts from the quality of your life. Your work should interest you, energize you and be rewarding. However, it should still leave time for you to enjoy other aspects of your life, such as your family, friends, hobbies and other interests.

To find out if work is where your balance falters, answer these questions:

- Do you feel like no matter how hard you work, you can never clear the paperwork off your desk?

- Do you have a problem remembering the last time you had a good laugh at the office?

- When you get home, do you feel physically and emotionally drained?

- Do you take work home and spend all night and weekends working on it?

- Do you have a reputation among your friends and family for always cancelling at the last minute?

- Do you put off playing with your kids because work comes first?

- Are you always missing special events because you need just 30 minutes more to catch up on work before you leave?

If you answered "yes" to these, you may be at the point where work is taking over your life and you need to start working on realigning your balance. And I know because I was a worst case offender. It makes me shake my head, sitting back now and thinking of all those times I sacrificed quality time with my family because work had to be done. Don't get me wrong, there were legitimate times when work had to, and still does need to, take priority, but in my case, I think my pride and ego got in the way much of the time. The more time I spent putting work ahead of my family, the more my psyche was getting warped into thinking that time spent furthering the business at my family's expense was the right and justified thing to do. After all, I was doing it for them. I was the one making the big sacrifice. I was a martyr!

What a load of... well, you know what. I actually recall times when I would get angry at my wife or kids for wanting to spend time with me.

How dare they?! I would think. *Didn't they realize what I was doing for them? They were the ones who would benefit from all my extra hours at work.*

I probably said this so many times to myself that I believed I was the only one suffering from my neglect.

A few weeks ago, I attended the high school graduation of my 18 year old daughter, Hannah. As I rushed up to the stage to catch that perfect moment on camera as she was handed her diploma, I was overwhelmed with pride and joy, as any parent should be. Eighteen years had passed in an instant. As a "hurray" went up from the crowd and she smiled at me, I realized how lucky I was that my wife and children stuck by me as I struggled to learn the true meaning of balance.

I'm proud to say that yesterday, when I got home from work (early), that my son, Evan, asked me to take him out on the river. "Absolutely!" I said. At 21, with friends to hang out with and girls to chase, he still wants to spend time with his old man. These are the incredible benefits of finding life balance that I'm grateful for.

Work isn't the only area where people fall out of balance though. For some it could be not taking enough time to be physically, spiritually or even mentally healthy. A tool that I find useful in assisting me in quickly and easily assessing the areas in my life that are most in need of attention is the Life Balance Wheel.

Think of the Life Balance Wheel as a giant sun shining rays of light into life's different, making sure they are not left in the shadows. In astrology, the sun represents the self. It is symbolic of directed will and a sense of purpose. The Life Balance Wheel can help you direct your awareness to the areas of your life that most need it.

The Wheel consists of four basic areas: physical, mental, emotional and spiritual. Each encompass a variety of factors in your life, as you can see in the diagram below. In the middle of the circle is you. When the wheel is completely round, you are balanced.

Using a sheet of paper and a pen, I want you to draw your own Life Balance Wheel.

A Balanced Approach to Life

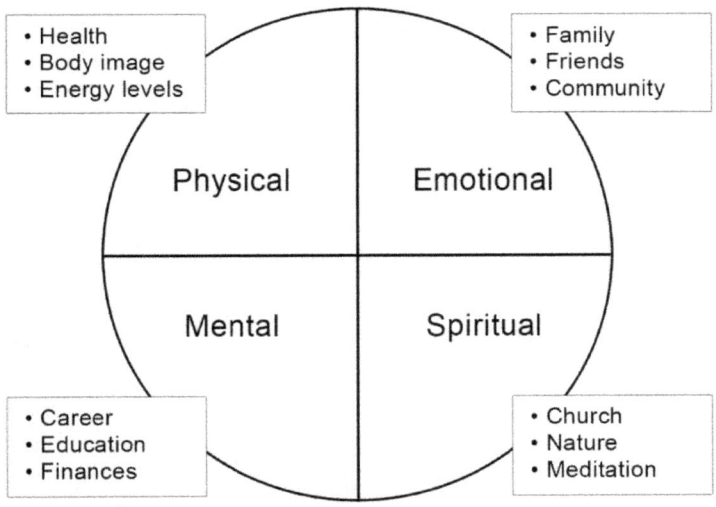

In each of the four sections of the wheel, I want you to include the different factors in your own life that fall into that category. Once you have your wheel drawn, honestly assess how happy you are in each of the four areas. For example, if you are unhappy with your physical appearance or health, put a mark halfway towards the outer edge of the circle, indicating you are out of balance and need to spend more time working on your physical self. If it makes it easier, you could also use a scale of 1 to 10. See the image of the Balance Wheel below as an example to guide you in this task.

Life Balance Wheel Example

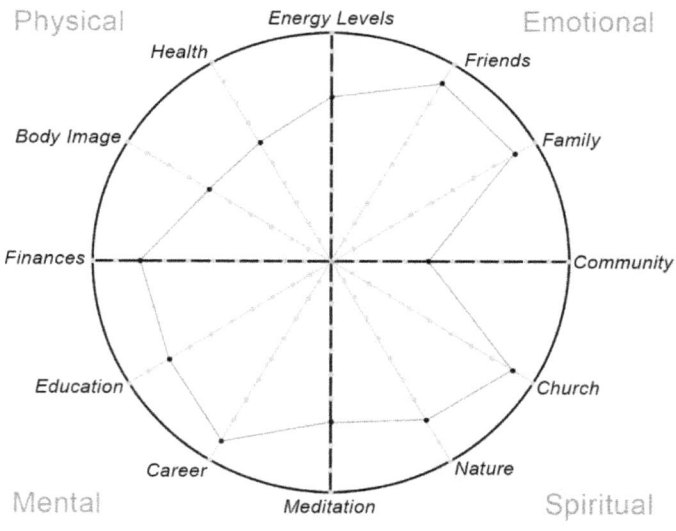

Ask yourself the following fifteen questions to make this process easier. They cover the physical, emotional, mental and spiritual aspects of your life.

1. How is your support network?
2. How strong are your friendships?

3. Do your interpersonal skills need work?
4. Do you get along with your parents, siblings, children and/or spouse?
5. How satisfied are you with your profession?
6. Do you enjoy what you do?
7. Do you spend an appropriate amount of time at work?
8. Do you find time for hobbies?
9. Do you have ways to relax and have fun?
10. Do you have too much debt?
11. Are you saving for the future?
12. Do you continue to find ways to improve your life and grow?
13. Do you find yourself mentally challenged?
14. Do you find yourself struggling with meaning in your life?
15. Do you have a sense of purpose?

When you have finished marking each section, join all the marks with a line and see how balanced (or unbalanced) your wheel is. You now have a visual representation of what areas in your life require more consideration and what you are doing well. This is an exercise you can repeat anytime you start feeling out of balance.

Think of your Life Balance Wheel like the tire on a car. If the tire is a little flat, how does it affect the performance of the car? It reduces gas consumption, the car pulls to the right and the ride gets rougher. You could choose to ignore it, however, at some point that tire is going to end up flat and you'll find yourself stranded on the side of the road or in an accident.

Your life is the same way. If one area of your wheel is flat, it will impact other areas of your life. If you don't feel good about your physical appearance, emotionally it will bring you down because you're not enjoying who you are. This lowered self-esteem may stop you from going out and socializing with others or exploring new opportunities. When you don't work on the full circle, you impact your performance in life. Don't wait to get sidetracked by a flat; you should be regularly checking the areas of your life to prevent problems beforehand.

When striving to achieve balance in your life, remember these three principles.

Principle 1: Balance is not time dependent

A good balance does not mean spending an equal amount of time in all four areas of the Life Balance Wheel. For example, it is impossible to spend 8-10 hours at work and be able to devote an equal amount of time at home with your family. Balance doesn't come necessarily from the amount of time you spend, but from the quality of time you spend.

So instead of sitting in front of the TV with your kids each night, mind numbingly watching another sitcom, turn the TV off and go for a walk, play a board game or simply talk. My wife and I made a commitment to go on a date once a week in order to spend more quality time with one another. We go to the movies or out to dinner, sometimes it's as simple as a cup of coffee and a walk. The important thing is it is a conscious decision we have made to invest time in each other.

Principle 2: Balance is about fluidity

In order to achieve a successful balance, you need to understand that it will vary over time. The right balance for today may not meet your needs next week, next month or next year. It all depends on what is happening in your life at any particular moment in time. If you're single, your demands will be different than if you're married or if you have children or if you are starting a career or ending one.

Frank Herbert said, "There's no secret to balance. You just have to feel the waves." It is a matter of assessing your life periodically and finding what is right for you in order to bring happiness and fulfillment into it at that point of time. You need to be flexible and learn how to adjust. Your Life Balance Wheel will help you with this task.

Your own observation skills will help you maintain fluidity as well. Watch and listen to the actions and words of those around you. Are they unsure whether asking you to do something might be an inconvenience to you? Do they always ask you things in a tone that expects an "I'm too busy" response? Does the family dog not even bother to come over for a tummy rub anymore? Managing fluidity to achieve balance is about recognizing when you are falling into old habits or creating new bad habits. It's about being aware of routine and not becoming so comfortable that you are unwilling to change even when you need to in order to grow.

Principle 3: There's no right answer for balance

There's no one perfect way to achieve a balance between the different areas in your life. There are just different ways. As the old adage says, "Different strokes for different folks." We all have different priorities and goals. The best balance is the one that works for you.

While there is no right answer, it is possible to build a proper foundation. Your balance should depend on two factors: completion and enjoyment. When you understand, adopt and practice these they will have a huge impact on your life.

As humans, we are creatures of completion, as we discussed earlier. It gives us a sense of accomplishment. It builds our self-esteem and confidence. Think about your to-do lists. If you write one with ten things on it and by 11 a.m. you have seven done, I bet you feel pretty good about the day. Your completion rate is connected to your contentment with your life. However, if at the end of the day, you've only finished one of the ten, and then must do the other nine the next day with all your other tasks, your outlook on tomorrow is already dismal. Completion creates assurance. It creates satisfaction. In order to keep your balance on par, you need to strive for completion in all areas of your life.

The other day I had a to-do list as long as my arm. Perhaps it was too ambitious of me, but I thought that I could get it all done. Scratch that, I *knew* I could get it all done. However, I miscalculated the amount of time I would end up spending on all the small things that popped up throughout the day. I ended up having to go to the bank. An employee was having trouble with a project. My daughter needed me to run home and get her gym clothes. To make a long story short, I didn't even finish a quarter of the things on my list.

Needless to say, I wasn't feeling too satisfied with my day when I walked through the door that night. I didn't even notice my two pups, tongues flapping and tails wagging, waiting at the door. I spent the entire evening trying to get more work done, much to the chagrin of my wife and kids who wanted me to spend time with them, and then I wasn't able to sleep because I couldn't stop thinking about all the things I needed to do the next day.

Do you see how not being able to complete my tasks at work during the day meant that I didn't spend the time I needed on myself and my family in the evening thus throwing my balance off? Even though I am fully aware of the importance of maintaining balance in my life, I still have to work hard at not falling into my old habits of putting work before my family.

Vice versa, sometimes it is the incomplete tasks or activities at home that affect the other areas of our life, such as not paying a bill or not making up after a fight. Completion is a fundamental part of creating and maintaining balance.

When I speak of enjoyment, you might think I'm referring to having a good time. By all means, having a good time is important to life; however, in relation to balance, that doesn't quite hit the mark. Enjoying life means taking pride in yourself, satisfaction in what you do, happiness in your day, celebration of life events, love in your relationships and a sense of well-being.

Completion and enjoyment go hand in hand. You can have a successful day, but not enjoy it. Or you can enjoy your day, but not complete anything that will move you towards your goals. Either will leave you feeling lopsided. The pressure of living a one-sided life is why so many successful people are not as happy as they could be.

Work, love and play are all intricate components of a balanced life. Without all three, you will always find your life lacking fulfillment. What's a job well done if you don't have someone to go home and share it with?

I wholeheartedly believe that what you look for you will find. Our brains are hardwired like that, so if you program it to seek out certain information, it will begin to look for it. We all know this is true. Think about when you first start dating someone new, all you look for is the exciting things in the relationship. At the beginning they are easy to find because everything is novel. Then, as the relationship progresses, the annoying little habits start to creep in. You know what I'm talking about, the nail chewing, the smacking at dinner, the way they leave their jacket on the floor when they walk in the door. The more you look for them, the more these little habits can transform into BIG annoying habits that have the potential to become deal breakers.

You have to choose what you want to look for based on the outcome that you want. What if your goal for every day was simply: I will complete something today and I will enjoy something? What if you woke each day and said that? What if you took that one step further and applied that statement to all the areas of your Life Balance Wheel? Would that kind of focus bring more balance into your life? Absolutely. If you do that every day, I guarantee you will have a good life. And the great part is it is easy and simple to implement.

If you're already in a situation where you are struggling with balance (perhaps too much time at work and your kids are yelling "stranger!" when you walk in the door at night), here are two tips that will help you start moving in the right direction:

Learn to Say "No"

Learning to say "no" graciously is an important tool for maintaining balance in your life. It is not possible for you to be everything to everyone. It is important for you to learn how much of yourself you can give away before you start getting worn down. When you reach that point, you need to be able to resist the urge to give a little more.

You must identify your priorities each day and act on them accordingly. Every time you say "yes" to one task, you are saying "no" to something else. Make sure you choose the right things to say "yes" to in your day. These should be the things that bring contentment and satisfaction into your life.

Remember, your new philosophy is to complete one thing and enjoy one thing every day, ensure you make time to do that by gracefully declining to do things that won't help you reach these goals.

Eliminate Time-Stealers

Be vigilant throughout your day about where you spend your time. Don't get caught up in bad habits that don't add value to your work or your life outcomes. Sometimes we just do things because we've always done them. If you think a person or a task is taking up your time unnecessarily, ask yourself: Is this a valuable use of my time? Does it help me complete what I want to do today? Does it add enjoyment to my life? Where else could I be spending my time?

With a little thought, planning and practice, you can free up hours every week to spend on the things that matter to you most. You can choose to put balance in your life. Your thoughts and actions will dictate the results.

You cannot be at your best if you do not have balance in your life. Write these words down and post them where you can see them every day as a reminder of how important balance is:

What I do today is important because I will never have today again.

My parents always encouraged me to live by this motto. They said to keep balance between work, family life, play and time for myself. All these aspects of your life are important. If there is no balance with your family, you lose them emotionally, supportively, and even possibly as a family unit. If there's no balance with your work, you lose your perspective and focus. If there's no balance spiritually, you can lose your purpose. And if you have no balance with yourself, you forget who you are and struggle each day, asking yourself: *Why do I do what I do?* Who you are is a combination of all these things and more. Thomas Merton said that happiness is not a matter of intensity, but of balance, order, rhythm and harmony. You need to find your own harmony within your life to achieve happiness.

Use the Life Balance Wheel to determine the priorities that need to be high in your life right now. Tell yourself you're going to complete something and enjoy something each day. Break the routines and bad habits that prevent you from having the balance in your life you so rightly deserve. Make the decision to restore your life. It is yours to enjoy and thrive in. You always have that choice. And remember; take a little time to romp with the dogs.

"Continuity gives us roots; change gives us branches, letting us stretch and grow and reach new heights."
- Pauline R. Kezer

CHAPTER TWO: REbuild Your Resilience

Napolean Hill once said, "The strongest oak of the forest is not the one that is protected from the storm or hidden from the sun. It's the one that stands in the open where it is compelled to struggle for its existence against winds and rains and scorching sun."

So it is with people. The people most comfortable and at one with themselves are not the ones who live with no challenges or adversity, they are the ones who have faced hardships and difficult times and pulled through. Not only have they pulled through, they have learned and grown from those experiences.

Take a moment and think about the following people:

- A politician who was defeated from political office seven times.

- A band that was turned down for a contract when the studio proclaimed "We don't like their sound and guitar music is on the way out."

- An actor who was forced to take a job that required him to dress as a giant chicken in order to get by.

- A writer whose first children's book was rejected by 23 publishers.

- A baseball player who struck out more than any player in the history of the game, 1330 times.

No one would have looked down on these people for giving up on themselves and their dreams in these circumstances. But none of them did, they chose to keep on going, to face the hard times and grow from them, and thankfully they did. Without their ability to weather the storm, we wouldn't have known Abraham Lincoln, The Beatles, Brad Pitt, Dr. Suess or Babe Ruth. They refused to surrender their dreams. Their personal resilience allowed them to continue on despite disappointment after disappointment. You too, can do this.

The great thing about personal resilience is that it is a skill you already possess; you just need to learn how to develop it. It is about creating the right habits and training it to come to the surface.

Years ago I heard Ian Percy, a motivational speaker, tell a story that puts resilience into perspective for most people. He related it to a tube of toothpaste. I bet, in your bathroom drawer, you probably have a tube of toothpaste that has been used much longer than the manufacturer ever anticipated it would. You've squeezed it and twisted it trying to get every little bit out that was left behind. You may have put it on the edge of the counter in order to get more leverage. I've actually had someone tell me that they would cut the tube open and scrape their toothbrush along the inside to get more toothpaste. Some of you may have even done the ultimate desecration (you know who you are) and jabbed the bristles of your toothbrush into the end to get the last remaining bits.

Does this sound familiar? The only way you can make a commitment to buying a new tube of toothpaste is to take the old one and throw it into the garbage. At this point you tell yourself that you will pick up a new one on the way home from work. Ultimately, you'll find the same thing happens every time. Here you are standing in front of the mirror that night, all ready for bed in your pajamas. You go to brush your teeth and you realize you forgot to pick up that new tube of toothpaste. You look down into the garbage can. There lies the old tube of toothpaste. *Perhaps*, you think as you gingerly fish it out of the can and blow the hair off the end of it, *I could squeeze out just a little bit more.*

And there always is just a little bit more. Think of that tube of toothpaste in terms of resilience. You are the tube of toothpaste. You always have just a little bit more to give. Do you ever find that just when you think you're done, you can dig down and find just a tad more energy to give? As a human being, you are virtually inexhaustible. Once you have accepted this, the question becomes: Is it your choice? Do you have control over the amount of energy you give? Or are you running on pure survival instinct?

Many times we go through challenges in our lives that leave us feeling drained, squeezed or scraped out. I hope you never, ever feel tossed aside. The key to becoming truly resilient is being able to fill the tube on your terms. You need to be able to be proactive with the way you go about using your energy so that you are ready to bounce back from the problems life throws at you. This way you'll never have to worry about being used up.

Often when you are stretched thin, you'll find that your body and mind will almost take on separate entities. Doctors, nurses, soldiers and parents with young children have all experienced this phenomenon, this sense of detachment. It's like driving home when you're tired at night. Have you ever driven the whole way and then not remembered any of it? In this case your body is taking over while your mind rests. Or awakening at 3 a.m. in the morning to the cries of a newborn babe, your mind automatically hears that cry and clicks on knowing that you need to get out of bed, pick up the baby, get the bottle, warm it up… Your body drifts along with you, carrying you about the tasks, but is never fully awake.

While this is a great survival mechanism, you work better when both your mind and body are at one. Spend too much time in one or the other condition and you will never realize your full potential. You need to make sure you change your routines and habits so you don't spend all your time in either state of being.

I find that change causes so much discomfort in people. Years ago, I heard the phrase, "Change is inevitable; growth is optional. Choose wisely." You will face change in your life, in order to survive, you must learn to grow and adapt to this change. Parents with newborns are always told to nap while the baby sleeps during the day so they won't be so sleep-deprived during the night. This one small change will make them more alert, attentive and all-around better caregivers.

You must learn how to deal with the day-to-day worries that wear you down, such as work stress, family commitments and financial troubles, as well as how to build a strong support system for dealing with possible traumatic events that could happen in your life, such as the death of a family member. By being proactive and building up your resiliency now, you can prevent the negative effects of stress and anxiety. It is too difficult to develop resiliency whilst in the middle of a traumatic event, think of it as trying to learn how to swim when you are already drowning.

Two things I always tell people to keep in mind when it comes to resilience, is that everything has an end and that most of us make our own emergencies. For the former, when you are in the middle of a difficult situation that you don't think will ever end, take a deep breath and say to yourself "And this too shall pass." And, with time, it will

For the latter, Richard Carlson sums it up wll in his book, *Don't Sweat the Small Stuff*. He says, "The first step to becoming a more peaceful person is to have the humility to admit that in most cases you're creating your own emergencies. Life will usually go on if things don't go according to plan. It's helpful to keep reminding yourself and repeating the sentence, 'Life is not an emergency.'"

Once you have these two things firmly implanted in your mind, you will have the foundation to easily build up your resilience.

With this new attitude towards resilience, I want to now share with you my Ten Commandments of Personal Resilience that will help you bounce back from adversity in your life. These are simple things you can incorporate easily into your schedule. With them you will increase your ability to deal confidently with situations that create stress and discomfort. Once you have these tools, nothing will stop you from reaching your someday.

R: Rely on Your Positive Attitude

I think teenagers are a lovely example of what happens when this commandment isn't followed. Anyone who has ever been in close contact with one of these creatures knows what I'm talking about. Many teenagers have a habit of being a little more negative than most people and due to this they have a tendency to blow the smallest things out of proportion.

My dad taught me the importance of having a positive attitude one day when I was a teen. I'm not sure if it sunk in at the time, but I value it now. I was probably 16 or 17 at the time, a wonderful age for parents and I had just come downstairs for breakfast. I was in a mood (no surprise) and, I'm ashamed to say, I kept picking on my mother. About everything. The food, the laundry, what we were doing that day. The entire time I was persecuting my poor mother, my dad sat at the other end of the table reading his paper. He let me continue on in this way for another few minutes before he set his paper down on the table and looked at me. I should have known at that point to shut my big mouth, but like I said before, I was in a sour mood. Slowly he flipped a few pages of the paper, folded it in half so the inside of the page was facing outward, twisted it into a roll, walked around the table and smacked the paper down in front of me with a resounding thump.

"Hey" I shouted, "What did you do that for?"

"Look," he said, pointing at the page he'd flipped it to, the obituaries.

"What am I looking for?" I said staring at the page.

"Your name!" he said. "If you don't see it in here then it must be a pretty good day, so you better start acting like it!"

I cannot stress enough how important a positive attitude is to the outcome of your day. Remember Winnie-the-Pooh's friend Eeyore, the old gray donkey? He was never happy. It didn't matter what came his way or what happened during the day, everything in his life was painted in shades of grey. It was bad news all the time. I believe if we're not careful, we can become like Eeyore. Worse yet, we can begin to attract Eeyore's to us. If you project negativity, you will attract negative people. The more you get used to being positive about the normal aspects of your life, the more likely you will remain optimistic when you are faced with negative situations.

The whole idea about being more positive is to make the choices that help you become more upbeat. One of the easiest things you can do to help with this is to keep a success journal. If you haven't used one before, I encourage you to start today. A success journal is merely somewhere you write down the good things happening to you and that you deem successes. You don't need anything to start, just a notebook, a pen and a willingness to look positively at the things going on in your life right now.

Here are a couple of tips you can use to get the ball rolling and make it easier for you to get started on your own journal:

1. Write in it just before you go to bed because then your mind will have only good things to focus on while you are sleeping.

2. Only write what you accomplished, succeeded with or what you were really proud of yourself for doing that day.

3. Read it again and again. Read several different dates before you go to sleep and your mind will dwell all night long on how great you are.

What a wonderful way to wake up each morning. Throughout my career I have encouraged and coached many people to use success journals. I can't tell you how many times these individuals have told me what an incredible turning point it was in their lives.

Another way to increase your positive attitude is to include more humor in your life. A lot of the time when something happens to us, we choose to see the negative side of it. However, often there is also a funny side as well. Why not try embracing this more often. Much loved and great comedian Bill Cosby once said, "Through humor, you can soften some of the worst blows that life delivers. And once you find laughter, no matter how painful your situation might be, you can survive it."

We always tell our kids not to cry over spilt milk. Why not use this philosophy in your own life. The next time something goes awry in your day and your first instinct is to respond negatively, ask yourself if you are getting upset over spilt milk. If you are, put a smile on your face and laugh it off. The more you can do this, the more able you will be to deal with the big stuff that comes your way. Remember, it is all about changing and growing. Within growth, you will find happiness with yourself.

E: Enjoy Life

Enjoying life is about learning to live. When I talk about enjoying life, I always like to tell the joke about the three construction workers having lunch. Maybe you've heard it. If not, I'll fill you in. Three construction workers, part of a crew building a skyscraper, were sitting around on the job site one day eating their lunch.

The first construction worker was complaining that all he ever got was bologna sandwiches. "I'm so sick of bologna," he said. "If I get one more, I'm going to jump off this building tomorrow."

The second construction worker was also dismayed with his lunch. "All my wife ever packs me is peanut butter and jam sandwiches! I'll jump too if I get another one."

The last construction worker said, "All I ever get is ham. I'm sick of them! I'm going to jump off with you guys if I get another ham sandwich."

The next day, the first construction worker opened his lunch box and found a roast beef sandwich. The second construction worker was happy to find a turkey sandwich. The third construction worker opened his lunch pail, sighed as he pulled out yet another ham sandwich and jumped off the building.

As the other two construction workers munched their sandwiches, the second one said to the first one, "You know, that's really sad."

"Yeah, it's too bad his wife just didn't pack him something different," said the first one.

"That's just it. He doesn't have a wife."

Now this is meant to be just a funny little joke, but even in real life we sometimes feed ourselves a lot of ham sandwiches even when we are capable of making something else. You *can* let your life be touched by positive energy and see the good that is right in front of you. You *can* find things to laugh and smile about and people to connect with each day. You are surrounded by blessings that you should start taking the time to be grateful for. Many people take the small things that make life worth living for granted, don't be one of them. Appreciate what life offers you each day.

When you can change your thinking from negative to positive, you will begin to believe in yourself and live each moment to its full extent. You need to pack your personal lunch box every day with things you can use to enjoy your life more. If you can find laughter and joy each day, you will be a healthier and wiser person. If you can find the little surprises life has to offer and reasons to hope, you will be a more balanced person. The best thing about this is that you can empower yourself to do it. You can be a person who makes the choice to live your life to its fullest.

My dogs know how to enjoy the little things and they're happier than any person I know. A walk down the road. Taking a nap in the sun on a warm summer afternoon. A tasty treat before dinner. Any one of these things can make their day. They don't mull over the past or worry about the future, they live fully in the moment. Are you a person who see's joy in the moment? You can be. Go ahead and feed your soul more than just ham sandwiches.

Life is all about enjoying the things we already possess and going out of our way now and then to expand our boundaries and experience new and different things. We persuade kids to try new things all the time. How often have you said, "How will you know if you'll like it or not if you won't try it?" We encourage them to try different sports, different activities, different programs, just so they can experience the world.

As adults, somewhere along the way we forgot this important lesson. Enjoying life is about getting yourself out of your routine, out of the rut. Remember to add little changes to your day to help break you free of the normal routines that hold you down. This could be driving home a different way, taking a class or simply having a different sandwich for lunch. It doesn't have to be big, just as long as you are doing something you wouldn't normally do. Enjoying life is about coming out of your comfort zone.

As adults we must learn to see each day anew, with fresh eyes to be able to spot enjoyment opportunities. We must break the invisible chains that bind us to lives of boredom and routine. Routine often masquerades as safety because it feels familiar; it hides itself in our comfort zones.

Don't misunderstand me; if your life is filled with joy and happiness because of the routine you have established, then I take my hat off to you. Enjoyment and happiness are defined differently from person to person.

But beware of the excuses built into routine. Don't let false enjoyment undermine your opportunities for happiness. Just because you don't experience many downs, crises or emergencies doesn't mean you're living your life to its full potential. Safety and comfort do not necessarily equate to enjoyment and happiness. I can be comfortable on my couch each day, but I could be much happier if I visited friends, took a walk with my wife or played a game with my kids. I could be expanding my horizons and experiencing something new and enjoyable if I took a course at the local college. There are always other options out there.

Don't be lulled into living a meek, passive life when you can do so much more. It's through feeling alive that you are able to build your resilience. This way, when you are faced with trying times, it is much easier to not let them overwhelm you because you know life has good things to offer and you have experienced them. When you are in difficult times you can think of the good things you want to enjoy again in your life and will work harder to overcome challenges to experience them.

S: Surround Yourself with a Healthy Environment

One of the biggest mistakes people make in their lives is accepting the environment that they are in as predetermined. You always have a choice. When I speak of environment, I include two factors: your physical surroundings and your relationships. Let's look at the latter first. You need to envelope yourself with healthy relationships; only have people in your life that believe in you and encourage you.

Ever wonder where the term "crabby" came from? It's not just because crabs have hard, scaly shells and so do most crabby people. Crabs will physically keep one another down. There's a story about a little girl at the beach with her father that illustrates this well. She used a little pail to capture a crab on the sand. Her father came down and asked her if she wanted to go for a swim.

"Daddy, I can't go for a swim," she said forlornly.

"Why not?" he asked.

"Because I have a pet crab here and every time I put him in the bucket and try to leave, he crawls out and tries to get away," she explained.

The father thought for a few seconds and then said, "Wait here" and walked down the beach. He returned a few minutes later with another crab and dropped it into the bucket with the other one.

"Okay," he said, "Now, let's go for that swim."

The girl looked into the bucket, confused.

"Dad, why is it okay to go now?"

"Look into the pail, sweetheart," he told her.

What the little girl saw in the pail is consistent with crabs. As one crab tried to climb out of the pail, the other one would grab it and pull it down, walk over its back and try to get out of the pail itself. The first one would then grab it and pull it down and the cycle continued with neither crab able to escape, when independently they would have no problem getting free.

Ask yourself this question: Do you have people in your life who are holding you back from trying the things you want to do? Do they keep you in a state of denial and frustration? Or do you have people who want the best for you and will support you when you want to change?

You already know the people in your life who are crabs. They are the ones who when you're spouse picks up the phone and, covering the receiver, whispers, "It's 'so and so!'" your mind immediately begins flipping through your rolodex of excuses to get out of talking to them. Or if you are fortunate enough to have call display, you may be in the habit of checking it as calls come in and if you see the name of one of the crabs in your life, you don't answer.

Crabs may come into your life inadvertently, but once you've identified them as crabs, people who don't support you or are negative all the time, you must make the decision to distance yourself from them as much as possible. Crabby people suck the energy out of you that you need to invest in being a more positive person.

W. Dayton Wedgefarth said this about a true friend, "I talk to him when I'm lonesome like; and I'm sure he understands. When he looks at me so attentively, and gently licks my hands; then he rubs his nose on my tailored clothes, but I never say naught thereat. For the good Lord knows I can buy more clothes, but never a friend like that." Of course, he was describing his dog, but isn't this the type of friends you need in your life? One who listens and encourages you, no matter what path you decide to go down? You need to eliminate the crabs in your life, bring in more dogs instead.

Besides building good relationships, the other important factor for your continued growth is to ensure you are living in the right type of environment that promotes a healthy lifestyle. Take the time to look closely at your home and work surroundings. Do they contain positive messages and information, such as pictures that inspire you or greenery? Is there lots of natural light? Do you keep healthy food within reach? Is it organized and clean? You need to constantly be looking at your environment because it will either hold you in the state you're currently in and increase your frustrations or it will allow you to expand and grow, seeing the possibilities available in your life.

I know when my office reaches a certain state of disrepair where the desk is piled high with folders, papers and books it makes it difficult for me to concentrate. I find myself struggling to find what I need to do my work, or a clear place to write. Eventually, I find myself staring at my computer, not getting much of anything done. However, if I take the time to clear out the mess and organize my space I feel refreshed and much more enthusiastic about my work.

I also try to keep my office full of things that inspire me. As discussed in *The Orange Popsicle*, my personal mission statement is posted above my computer where I can see it every day. I have several motivational posters on the walls and many, many pictures of my family. I keep souvenirs that I've picked up on vacation on my shelves, along with my much loved Disney memorabilia. And of course, a couple photos of my mutts. When I find myself lacking incentive during my day, I simply take a couple minutes to look at the things I love and it rejuvenates me. Does your home and office do this for you? If your space doesn't make you feel good about your life, perhaps it's time for a little redecorating.

I: Improve Your Coping Skills

Confucius said "Our greatest glory is not in never falling, but in rising every time we fall." The only way this is possible is if you have good coping skills. To maintain strong personal resiliency, you need to take a proactive approach and maintain these skills.

From a young age, you learn how important coping skills are to life. If you had siblings, you know just how hard it is to ignore teasing or hair pulling. Even as an adult, you may still have to deal with this to some degree (hopefully, you don't have to deal with the hair pulling!).

It's important to understand this during downtimes. Remember the saying no one gets through life alive? Joking aside, it is no coincidence that most people relate life to a roller coaster ride. There are ups and there are downs. You don't get to have the excitement without some of the heartache. I've found that it is in the heartache that you grow the most. That you find what you are really made of.

Accomplished speaker and writer, Charlie "Tremendous" Jones is a good example of how improving your coping skills and refusing to back down will improve you and your life. After over 5000 seminars and over 1.5 million copies of his book, *Life is Tremendous* in print, Jones said he has had more failures than successes, but no one remembers the failures. After selling for over 76 years, he has found that two words from his youth have resonated in everything he's done, "I will." Throughout the many predicaments he's found himself in, he's come out the other side by "growing through it."

Jones said, "Things don't go wrong and break your heart so you can become bitter and give up. They happen to break you down and build you up so you can be all you were intended to be."

One of the simplest ways to enhance your coping skills is to practice relaxation techniques. You can sign up for a meditation class or just block off some quiet time for yourself, about 20 minutes a day where you can sit and take time to evaluate your life. Or you can go for a walk outside (your dog would love this!) to rejuvenate yourself. You need to develop the relaxation technique that works for you, whether this is deep breathing, taking in nature or writing. This type of mental preparation and training will keep you grounded and give you the ability to think clearly in emotionally draining situations.

Jane and I signed up for a meditation class together. We both found our jobs were becoming hectic and we were quickly finding that the work stress was creating an imbalance in our lives. Meditation allowed us to share quality time together while strengthening our coping skills. It was a funny sight to see us going out the door in our exercise wear toting pillows and blankets in the early evening. I wondered what the neighbors thought of this, they being much more accustomed to seeing me with a briefcase in my hand than a yoga mat.

I loved the meditation classes. They allowed me to quiet my mind and body. You don't realize how much a stressful environment is impacting you until you try and silence your thoughts. The additional benefit to this approach was that it enabled me to just enjoy being in the moment more. Even though the classes ended a while ago, I still practice the skills. Sitting on my deck, watching the water and listening to the sounds of nature around me allows me to escape the stress that creeps into my life. Appreciating what's good in life goes a long way to improving coping skills.

Physical activities and exercise are two other ways to expand your coping skills. This doesn't mean you need to run to the gym every day, it could be a brisk walk at lunch to clear your head, get your heart pumping and refocus yourself. You could join a sports team or do Pilates in the morning before starting your day.

If you struggle with commitment, find a friend or a colleague who wants to do the same thing and use each other to stay motivated in the activity of your choosing. Ongoing physical exertion will enable you to deal better with stressful situations that occur.

If you own a dog, they are an excellent gauge of your physical health. If your dog is fat, you're probably not getting enough exercise. As O.A. Battiste said, "A dog is one of the remaining reasons why some people can be persuaded to go for a walk." So, if you're not going to do it for yourself, do it for Rover.

Don't just think of exercise when it comes to physical activities either. You need to consider what you're putting into your body as well. Proper nutrition helps you deal with stress. Eat healthy foods in moderation. Feel free to still enjoy a meal out or a treat here and there, but do cut back on junk food. Review what is going into your body and be aware of whether it is helping or hindering you. Chemicals and preservatives weaken your immune system and make it harder for you do deal with stress. Imagine you are what you eat, would you rather be green and lean like the bean or soft and pasty like a Twinkie? The bean can maintain its composure under a little pressure without breaking, but give the Twinkie even just a bit of a squeeze and you'll end up with a mess.

Another factor that affects your body is the amount of sleep you have each night. Most people are not getting the recommended amount. Deep, restful sleep repairs your body and revitalizes you for the next day. If you don't sleep enough or you have a restless sleep, your resistance begins to weaken. No matter how much you exercise or eat properly, if you don't get a suitable amount of sleep you will be ill-equipped for the day.

To help reduce the amount of restless sleep you are getting, make sure your bedroom is a relaxing environment. Try using black out blinds on windows, playing relaxation CD's and, at the very least, minimizing TV watching before bed. Never discuss finances or issues with family before going to sleep. You need to create the right habits to support a restful slumber. Arguing about money, fretting about what's going on at work or worrying about how your kids are doing at school will not promote the soothing atmosphere you need for good sleep.

The human body is an amazing thing; it will serve you well if you just keep up a proper maintenance schedule. Professional surfer Laird Hamilton appreciates the resiliency of his body. He has sustained hundreds of injuries in his career: broken bones, separated shoulders and, quote, holes in the head. "I don't think I'm indestructible," he said, "but God makes a pretty good car!"

Your body can carry you through most anything if you treat it right. Take the time to tune your own engine and put air in the tires. Do this and your body will take you a long way.

L: Look to Your Future

This is about having a vision for you. I'm sure you've heard of Bill Gates, if you haven't, where have you been living? He's the co-founder, chairman and former CEO of Microsoft Corporation, which is the world's leading provider of software for personal computers. Gates was once asked by *Fortune* magazine to explain the remarkable success of the company and he responded, "Our vision, which has not changed since the day the company was founded." That vision led his company and continues to lead the company to its continuing achievements and growth.

In the words of Robert Fritz, "In the presence of great dreams, pettiness disappears. But in the absence of the great dream, pettiness prevails." When you don't have that vision for yourself, that great dream, it's easy to get caught up in the trivial things that hold you down.

If you want a real lesson in vision, pick up Victor Frankl's book, *Man's Search for Meaning*. Frankl was imprisoned in a concentration camp during the Holocaust. He was able to survive the emotional, mental and physical abuse because he believed he had something great still to accomplish in his life. He dreamt every day of standing at a podium in a warm auditorium and sharing his story with other people in order to help change the world.

You may find that your own vision comes to you during a traumatic or upsetting time. Often during these times you find strength and will in yourself that you didn't know you had. Elizabeth Kubler Ross, a psychiatrist and author of the groundbreaking book, *On Death and Dying*, once said "People are like stained-glass windows. They sparkle and shine when the sun is out, but when darkness sets in; their beauty is revealed only if there is light from within."

You may find it hard to have a clear dream in our chaotic world. Quiet time by yourself may give you the opportunity to find your dream. It will allow you to see things better than you've been able to in the past. Take the time to write your vision down. The more visible you can make it, the easier it will be to achieve. If it is what you want to see in your life, you will begin to look for opportunities to make it happen. Helen Keller, a symbol of resilience if there ever was one, said, "Worse than being blind is to be able to see and yet have no vision." We will discuss vision more further on.

I: Include Goal Setting

It's one thing to be able to dream, it's another thing entirely to put goals to those dreams. Often people become stuck in the someday honeys we discussed earlier. The problem with the someday honeys is that when you say, "Someday I'll do that" you're forcing it to stay a dream and are not adding any depth to it. That's what goal setting does. It creates focus to make the dream happen. Denis Waitley said that the reason most people never reach their goals is because they don't define them or ever seriously consider them as believable or achievable. Winners can tell you where they are going, what they plan to do along the way to get there and who will be sharing the adventure with them. Have the courage to take your dreams and start making them reality.

When setting goals, use the S.M.A.R.T system. Your goals should be Specific, Measurable, Achievable, Realistic and Timely. Follow these guidelines and you will always set goals you can meet.

E: Educate Yourself

You have the ability to expand your mind. And by expanding your mind, you increase your opportunities. If you're not creating new possibilities through knowledge, how can you produce solutions to challenges that crop up in life? If you try to solve new problems with old ways of thinking, you will run into the same roadblocks you always have.

Knowledge helps you think critically about situations. It gives you the tools to look at a situation you're facing and know that there is a better way. Remember that it is about choice. When you choose to educate yourself by reading books, watching documentaries or by taking a program, you're always expanding your mind. Your mind is pliable and it can grow to include whatever you want. The more information and knowledge that you have, the more tools you will have at your disposal and the more flexible you will become in life.

Think of young children, we are constantly teaching them new things in order to better their lives. As babies and toddlers we teach them to walk, how to talk and how to feed themselves. As they go through elementary school they learn math, science and English, all necessary for life. As teenagers, they learn how to drive, get a job and live on their own. When we are young it is natural to be learning. However, sometime after this we forget that we need to be continually updating our knowledge.

As you go through life you will encounter new situations and with these situations, you will need tools you may not have acquired. The key to resilience is to go out of your way before you end up in these situations to get the tools you need.

N: Navigate Through Worry

There's a phrase that says, "Worry is like a rocking chair. It gives you something to do, but it won't get you anywhere." We've all had sleepless nights where our problems keep churning in our mind and it doesn't do anything but make us tired in the morning. It doesn't solve problems. Only through action can we move past that worry state.

When I was a kid, we had one of those big trees in our neighborhood with limbs that stretched way out from the trunk. I was determined that one day I would master climbing to the top of that tree. Yes, my parents had warned me not to when I'd voiced my intent, telling me how dangerous it was, but it just kept calling my name, daring me to give it my best shot. I'd lie in the shade underneath its branches, just staring up through all those intertwining leaves and limbs, just imagining how great it would be to sit amongst them. Then that day came. My parents were out and my friend's parents, who lived beside us, with a clear view of the tree, were also gone. I was ready for an adventure and that tree was beckoning.

I told my friends that I was going to do it; I was going to climb that tree. Soon word got around and my two brothers and a small crowd of our friends had formed around it. As they watched, I masterfully shimmed up the trunk and grabbed hold of the first branch. I then slowly climbed my way from one branch to the next, moving further into the canopy of leaves. Soon, I had disappeared from sight. I could still hear the murmur of voices below, but I was enthralled with the experience. I had accomplished something none of them had been able to do. I was pretty proud.

As I neared the top, the branches thinned out and I stopped to catch my breath. Sitting on my perch I took a moment to relish the glory of my victory. I swore I could see clear across town from my vantage point. It was breathtaking. Then I glanced down and reality set in. I was high up. Really high up. I needed to get down NOW. With my heart pounding I started to inch my way through the branches. I could feel my legs shaking as I felt around for a foothold below me. I managed to get about half way back to the ground when I couldn't feel any more branches beneath me. I was stuck and afraid. I called to my friends for help. It was at this point that we realized we had a bigger issue. We were not to climb the tree and if any parent came home and found me in it, we were all going to be in big trouble.

My friends formed an impromptu huddle underneath the tree. As I watched them confer over the best way to get me down, every once in a while one glancing up at me, I tried my best not to imagine myself plummeting to my death. After a few minutes one of my brothers broke away from the rest and ran to the house. He came back carrying something underneath his arm that looked like a sweater. He showed it to the group and they all nodded in agreement. My other brother, craning his neck to see me, gave me the verdict.

"You're going to have to jump," he yelled.

"What?!" I cried. "Are you insane, I can't jump!"

"We've got a blanket," he informed me, and I saw my brother flipping the "sweater" open on the ground.

"What's that supposed to do?" I asked warily.

"Well, we're each going to take an edge and hold it like the firemen do," he said, "Then you'll jump in it and we'll catch you."

I mulled this over in my mind for minute. It didn't sound like much of a plan. Frankly, I thought they were all crazy, but I couldn't think of anything better.

"Ok," I called down. "I'll do it."

Easier said than done. Despite my decision to make the leap, I couldn't bring myself to release my death grip on the tree. I didn't think I would ever have the courage to do it. On the ground, my friends were all yelling, trying to coax me from the tree. It was my brother who gave me the encouragement I needed though.

"Dad's going to kill you if he catches you up there, you know!"

And I did know. The fear of getting caught, outbid my fear of getting hurt and I mustered up what little courage I had and made the leap.

I swear, for a brief moment I was sure I was flying. It was a fantastic sensation. But gravity has a way of knocking you back into reality and I plunged towards the ground.

To give my friends credit, they did manage to catch me. However, the force of me hitting the blanket caused some of them to lose their grip and I struck the grass with a thud that knocked my teeth together. Fortunately, I wasn't seriously hurt, just some bruises, sore muscles and one massively wounded ego.

It was an important lesson for me. If I had of let my worry of hurting myself overwhelm me, I may have been up in that tree all afternoon. Granted, my father probably wouldn't have killed me (and there's a possibility my decision to jump may have), but at the time it seemed a good likelihood that he would. I made the decision to do something about it. I looked at the worst case scenario, the end of my short life, and decided I'd chance it. I took control of my fear and therefore the outcome of what was happening and took action.

This is what you need to do in your own life. When you find yourself weighed down with worry and unable to take action, ask yourself what the worst case scenario is. Once you've answered this, ask yourself: *Can I live with that? Is it okay? Am I prepared for it?* Sit down even with a piece of paper and write it out. What exactly are you worried about? Next, write down what you can do about it. Think of all the options, actions or tasks that you can do personally to solve it. Think hard. Don't just accept the first idea that you come up with. Don't look for the fastest solution either. Brainstorm; let your mind wander and see what possibilities and options you can come up with.

Once you've done this, look carefully at everything on your paper and select one or two that will best help you deal with the situation. Now go out and act on these. The more you act, the less time you have to worry. The reason you worry is because you are not making decisions. You are handing over control of the situation to someone else. Remember, in life there is always a lot to think about, but nothing to worry about. As Albert Einstein said, "I never worry about the future. It comes soon enough."

C: Continue to Grow

It's easy to become stagnant and complacent. Continuing to grow means you need to generate awareness every single day of your life. You need to expose yourself to different opportunities, try different things and believe that there are greater things out there for you. You can create the life you want as long as you don't accept the status quo. Creating awareness is something you do internally. It is when you can say to yourself, *I've had enough of this situation. I want change.* Sometimes by putting yourself in new situations, you can produce this externally.

I bet at one point or another in your life, you had a goldfish that lived in a goldfish bowl. Goldfish face the same problems you and I have. Goldfish will grow to the size their environment will accommodate and then they will stop. The bowl itself dictates the size of the goldfish. It doesn't matter how many of those brightly colored flakes you feed them, how often you clean the bowl or how much you talk to them (don't worry, I won't tell), they will just stop growing. The fascinating thing is if you take the goldfish out of the bowl and put them into a larger aquarium, they begin to grow again. Even if they haven't grown in months, the second aquarium creates a bigger environment and it is a sign for the goldfish to start to grow again. And, once again, they will only grow to the size that the new aquarium dictates. At that point, they will stop again. Move the goldfish to a pond and the process starts all over.

You see, life teaches you lessons all the time. It is up to you to learn them. How big is your goldfish bowl? What opportunities can you take advantage of to grow the size of it? Challenge yourself every morning to create one new action that you can implement to kick start a change in your life that will make you grow. No matter how old or young you are, you can always learn and develop. Old dogs can learn new tricks.

E: Encourage Yourself and Others

You can't ever give up on life. You have to keep cheering yourself on. At the same time, you need to support other people in your life as well. I was taught that the sign of a winner is someone who loves winning situations whether it's their win or someone else's. I want you to find people who are winning and be the first one to run up to them and congratulate them. Let them know you are proud of them. By being positive, people will start to be positive as well and direct this towards you. The more positivity you attract, the more you will build up your resiliency.

And remember that it is just as important to encourage yourself and others when they are not succeeding as when they are. William Saroyan summed this up when he said, "A word of encouragement during a failure is worth more than an hour of praise after a success." Know that a word of encouragement given off chance by you could be the difference between success and failure for someone else.

Take one of these commandments at a time and begin to work on it. Whether it is developing a more positive attitude, setting goals, trying some relaxation techniques or just offering an encouraging word, choose one and put it into practice. The more you can build yourself up the better you will be able to handle the harsh conditions that life sometimes hands you. And not only will you be able to handle them, you will be able to prosper in them. Helen Keller said, "Character cannot be developed in ease and quiet. Only through experience of trial and suffering can the soul be strengthened, ambition inspired and success achieved."

"I imagine that yes is the only living thing."
- e.e. cummings

CHAPTER THREE: REimagine Your Life

Reimagne. A funny word. I hear it most when people say "Just imagine!" Lotto 6/49 has built an entire marketing campaign around this concept, asking people to imagine their lives with 5, 10 or 20 million dollars. A new home. A new car. A trip around the world. No financial worries. This is a matter of daydreaming for most and will become reality for only a lucky few.

However, imagining is more than just about money. You can always reimagine your life. Reimagining is about reclaiming feelings of joy, reigniting passion for who you are and the life you live and brining happiness back into your life. It's about regaining that "I'm going to take on the world" mentality, uncovering the "I'm going to do something great with my life" feeling that I know you have felt at some point in your life when your confidence was high and you weren't mentally, physically or emotionally drained by all the fear, doubt or distractions of life. You may have come to accept these as the truth and adopted them as normal occurrences, but you can reimagine your life without them.

To reimagine is to break the invisible chains that bind your greatness. It is about tearing down the walls that words of doubt have built between you and the person you want to be. To reimagine is to embrace the possibilities and opportunities life offers and use them to become the person you want to be.

Michelangelo, the gifted artist, once stated, "I saw an angel in the marble and carved until I set him free." He believed that every stone had a statue slumbering within the marble shell and it was the sculptor's task to discover it. So it is with all of us. In you is a great and beautiful person just waiting to be set free. Reimagine yourself as that person. Desire and action will liberate you. Don't fear the chisel and the hard work. Michelangelo said, "The greater danger for most of us lies not in setting our aim too high and falling short; but in setting our aim too low, and achieving our mark."

Parents are always telling their children to be the best they can be. My mom and dad were always telling me that I could be anything that I wanted. Your parents probably said the same. Remember that; when the world was at your fingertips? I'm sure you were encouraged to be whatever you wanted, whether that was a firefighter, an astronaut, or a doctor. The message was clear: dream and believe in the dream. I believed those words, that as long as I believed it and was willing to work hard to get it, I could be whatever I wanted.

I have to admit, I'm a dreamer. I like to spend time sitting on the porch, staring at the water and dreaming, dreaming of something more. Dreaming is one of the reasons why I created my company, Getting to Someday. No matter where my work took me, I would run into people using the same familiar phrase, "Someday I'm going to." Someday, someday, someday. I started to wonder what happened to the encouragement telling us to just go for it. Work hard and you will achieve it. Dream big. Remember how great that felt when you heard those words and knew you had the complete support and encouragement of people you love?

When I ask people if they've accomplished all they wanted in life, the things that they've dreamt of, the things that would bring great joy into their lives, I hear the same answers: "Life got in the way," "I have too many other responsibilities now" or "I just don't have time." Are you too busy living life to really live life?

Lives filled with vision and dreams are not for only a select few. They are a gift for everyone to enjoy. You need to choose to accept and open these gifts. Think about it. When you are caught up in routine, you find yourself in a rut. You continually sacrifice what you want for the demands of your work, the needs of your family or financial pressures. Think about the thoughts in your head and the feelings in your heart at these times. I can guarantee you were not engaged or embracing life.

Chances are you were tired, listless and frustrated. You may even have been bored, angry or impatient. Without reimagining your life to include your visions and dreams, you are just going through the motions.

In the movie *The Dead Poets' Society,* the teacher, played by Robin Williams, inspires his students by using the words "carpe diem," seize the day. This is what I want you to do. Reimagine yourself when you were a child heading out on the first day of school, standing at the end of the driveway with your little backpack and brand new shoes, looking down the street to catch the first glimpse of the big yellow school bus. You held your parent's hand tightly, but inside you were imagining a whole new world filled with fun and exciting things to discover and enjoy.

Reimagine the first day of your career, when you arrived untainted, unscathed by the business world and ready to make a real name for yourself. You were nervous about doing something wrong, but you had that unyielding faith that only those in their early 20's seem to have that you were going to accomplish big things. You were going to make a difference.

Reimagine your wedding day, your first real vacation, the birth of your child, an award you won. Reimagine the emotion, the thoughts that these events had on your life. Reimagine the excitement and joy these days brought you. Puts a whole new meaning on seize the day, doesn't it? And it all comes from having a dream for yourself, for having a vision of who you want to be and how you want to live.

I've witnessed the impact of vision on people of all ages, cultures and even perceived limitations. I place a big role on the ability to dream and make those dreams a realty. Look at Christopher Reeve, who played the role of mild-mannered reporter, Clark Kent and his alter ego Superman. An unfortunate accident left Reeve disabled in body, but not spirit. Although life threw him a curve, which I'm sure was not part of his vision; his unyielding desire and compassion to help others generated a new vision. He created the Christopher and Dana Reeve Foundation, which is dedicated to curing spinal cord injuries by funding innovative research and improving the quality of life for people living with paralysis through grants and information advocacy. He was a true Superman through his strength of vision and conviction. Reeve said, "I have never been disabled in my dreams."

Sometimes it takes a moment of disaster or near disaster to show us the importance of dreams. A wake up call if you will. We've all had one. They come disguised in many different forms: a stroke, a death in the family, a broken heart, the dreaded call in the middle of the night. I had my own and sometimes it still causes my hands to shake just thinking about it. I was driving home one day after visiting with a client when my cell phone rang. When I answered it, I could hear sirens on the other end and a stranger's voice was telling me that my wife and son had been in a bad car accident and I should get there quickly. It's hard to describe what I was feeling unless you've gone through a similar situation. My heart seemed to stop and pound at the same time. My mouth went try and a thousand things ran through my mind: *What would I find at the accident? Was everyone okay? Was my wife and son hurt? Or worse?*

When I finally made it to the scene, the Jaws of Life had been used to remove the door on the driver's side to free Jane and she was on her way to the hospital. I frantically looked around for Evan, but he was missing. Someone, thinking they were doing a good deed, had walked him a few blocks to where my daughter was at a birthday party because she didn't think he should see his mother in the state she was in. Unfortunately, I didn't even know about the birthday party, so there I was, looking at a mangled car and eager to get to the hospital to find out the extent of my wife's injuries, but with two missing children. For all I knew, my life was potentially changed forever.

The good news was I found my children about two hours later. While stressed and worried, my son had only sustained a few bumps and bruises from the accident. The bad news was that my wife had sustained five fractures in her pelvis and had to remain in a hospital bed at home for months while she healed.

We all hear of the importance of living life to the fullest possible extent, but sometimes it takes a wakeup call to acknowledge this and truly believe it. If you want more out of your life, you need to define your own personal vision for it and take the steps to achieve it. Vision is the foundation for all growth. If you want more out of life, you must clearly define what the "more" looks like or otherwise you find yourself standing at the starting blocks frustrated because you don't know where to go.

Remember the book *Alice in Wonderland*? Think back to when she first met the Cheshire Cat. She was walking down a road in the woods when she came upon a fork in it. She was unsure of what path to take so she asked the cat:

> "Would you tell me, please, which way I ought to go from here?" she asked the Cat.
> "That depends a good deal on where you want to get to," said the Cat.
> "I don't much care where— " said Alice.
> "Then it doesn't matter which way you go," said the Cat.
> "—so long as I get SOMEWHERE," Alice added as an explanation.
> "Oh, you're sure to do that," said the Cat, "if you only walk long enough."

If you don't have a vision for what you want, then chances are, you're spending a lot of time wandering around doing plenty of things, but are they the right things for you? For sure you'll end up somewhere, but with no idea as to where you are going, odds are you'll be disappointed with the destination, and have nothing more to show for your work than sore feet.

Without vision, without dreams, how can you be excited about life? I remember laughing when I was reading a quote from Winnie the Pooh which said, "The pilot light is out on my flame of ambition." *The pilot light is out on my flame of ambition.* Ha! How many times have you felt that way? A clear vision ignites passion and ambition. That's the way you were meant to live. If you want more passion and ambition in your life, take the time now to reimagine your life by creating a vision to start the flame.

Whenever I talk about vision, I refer to one of the greatest visionaries of all time, Walt Disney. Disney built the number one travel destination in the world and it was all based on a dream and a mouse. There were four words that Disney created his philosophy of life on. He said that you have to dream, believe, dare and do. Disney believed that it all started with a dream, with a vision. He defined the dream as a wish that only your heart makes. That's the emotional pull towards what you want from your life. It should be clearly defined. Once you have your dream, he said you needed to believe it. You need to unquestionably and implicitly believe that you can attain that dream.

As you gain that belief, you have to dare yourself to go out and accomplish the things that need to be done to make that dream a reality. Then you have to commit yourself to doing them. You can't back down just because it scares you. You can't fall into old habits. If you continually do what you've always done, you will continually get what you've always got. Disney understood this. You have to dream big first. Find out what you really want. Believe in it. Dare yourself to think differently. Act differently. True greatness comes in doing it every single day, ingraining the thoughts and actions into your habits.

Soon after the completion of Disney World, someone said, "Isn't it too bad that Walt Disney didn't live to see this?" Mike Vance, who is the Creative Director of Disney Studios replied, "He did see it. That's why it's here." That's the power of vision. Success starts with your dream and what is important to you. Never do people fail because of a lack of brain power, opportunity or potential. It's because they don't organize their energies around a definite vision.

Having a vision is a powerful thing. Throughout history you can see the impact of visions that call people to action. Great leaders use visions to inspire and motivate others. President John F. Kennedy had a vision of man landing on the moon by the end of the 1960s and, sure enough, in the summer of 1969, the whole world watched in amazement as Neil Armstrong took those first small steps. Before this point, no one could have imagined that someone would one day stand on the moon. Kennedy's clear vision and strong conviction empowered thousands of scientists, experts and engineers to work together non-stop developing the knowledge and technology that would achieve this vision. None of this would have happened without his ability to imagine someone walking on the moon. His vision created the energy and momentum that excited people and turned his dream into reality.

Another vision that moved a nation was Dr. Martin Luther King's civil rights aspiration. His "I have a Dream" speech, delivered on the steps of the Lincoln Memorial resonated with and moved millions of people to embrace an attitude of acceptance and equality for all. His speech awakened an entire population.

Kennedy and King were able to create powerful visions and communicate these visions to millions of people. These visions transformed a nation and greatly affected the whole world. If you believe in a vision enough, it has the ability to change not only your own life.

Look at Woodrow Wilson, the 28th president of the United States of America as an example. He was once asked, "How have you done so much in your lifetime?" And he replied:

> I grow great by dreams. I have turned my mind loose to imagine what I wanted to do. Then I've gone to bed and thought about my dreams. In the night, I dreamt about my dreams. And when I woke in the morning, I saw the way to make my dreams real. While other people were saying, "You can't do that; it is impossible," I was well on my way to achieving what I wanted.

I'm sure you've heard the phrase "what you see is what you get." Whatever your brain looks for, it will find. If you define your vision and see your vision, you will achieve your vision. You've probably said many times, "I'll believe it when I see it." I want you to rethink that phrase. Say to yourself, "I'll see it when I believe it." When you define your vision yourself, you will see it come true.

Psychologists tell us that nothing controls our lives more than our self-image. You live like the person you see in the reflection of the mirror. You are what you think you are. You become what you think of yourself. If you can't see yourself as successful, you won't be. If you can't imagine yourself happy, you won't be. You can't be it if you can't see it. Your success in life is limited to your vision. If you want to change your life, you must change your vision of your life.

You probably think a dog can't be anything other than a dog right? I mean, they have four legs, a tail and bark. They are good at lying on the couch, barking at strangers and playing fetch. This isn't true though, a dog can be a rescuer pulling drowning people out of the water, a dog can be a police officer sniffing out drugs, a dog can even be a paramedic, alerting people of impending seizures so they can take their medicine to prevent them. If a dog can be all these things, isn't it conceivable that you can be something you never thought possible?

Arnold Schwarzenegger was famous in the 70s for his physique and being the number one bodybuilder in the world. When he retired from bodybuilding, a newspaper reporter asked him, "What do you plan to do next?" The answer that Schwarzenegger gave the reporter shocked him. He said, "I'm going to be the number one movie star in Hollywood." At the time, it was hard to imagine how this large muscle man who was not a professional actor and who spoke poor English with a strong Austrian accent could ever hope to be the number one actor in a place filled with aspiring talent.

So the next logical question from the reporter was, "How do you plan to make this dream come true?" Schwarzenegger's response was profound. He said, "I'll do it the same way I became the number one bodybuilder in the world. What I do is create a vision of who I want to be. Then I start living like that person in my mind as if it were already true."

What you see is what you get. Not only did Schwarzenegger accomplish his vision of conquering Hollywood, but as we all know, he turned his vision to politics as well. Remember, if you can see it, you can be it.

You only get one life to live, so why not live the best life possible. What do you see for yourself? What more do you see yourself doing? Having a clear personal vision can help you leap over some of the most difficult hurdles in your life.

My children's great-grandmother is 97 years old. Twelve years ago she was diagnosed with cancer and told she had about six months left to live. The first thing she did was buy new patio furniture for the upcoming spring season and new orthotics for her shoes. When her family asked her why she would spend her money on these things when she only had a short time to live, her answer was simple, "That's what the doctor said. I don't have to accept that. I have to see my great-grandchildren graduate from school." You see, Nan was a teacher and valued education above all else because she saw it as a vehicle for success in life and there was no way she was going to miss out on seeing this for her great-grandbabies. The only thing the doctor had to say to her was, "Whatever you're doing, keep on doing it." Vision and positive attitude, what an incredible combination.

Let's go back to the phrase what you see is what you get. This is the Universal Law of Attraction. It is a simple concept, but requires practice. As you practice it, understand it and accept it, there is no going back. It will become part of your life. It is important to understand that the Law of Attraction is neutral. It plays no favorites. Whatever you believe, whatever you look for, good or bad, you will attract it to you. This is such an important point. Your vision of the future must be a positive one. You must define it, write it down and read it over and over again so the words and images are crystal clear in your mind. You get what you put your energy and focus on. The Universal Law of Attraction is working in your life right now whether you are aware of it or not. You're attracting people, situations, jobs and much more into your life.

Once you're aware of this law and how it works, you can start to use it deliberately to attract what you want. You must be very clear on exactly what you desire for your vision. Focus on it. Give it all your positive energy. Give it all your attention. See it, believe it and believe that you deserve it. Once you see it clearly and believe it, now *expect* to see it. Look for those things that support your vision and don't hesitate. Take action. If something fits your vision and feels right, then forge ahead and do it.

Always expect to see your vision come true. Expect great things to happen to you.

Let's look at the steps for creating your vision. First, you've got to really desire more in your life. This is that burning desire that gives you the courage to make change happen. Napoleon Hill, in his landmark book *Think and Grow Rich* said, "The starting point of all achievement is desire." Keep this constantly in mind. Weak desires bring weak results just as a small amount of fire makes a small amount of heat. Your first step in visioning and achieving your dreams is you must really want to achieve them.

Second, see yourself achieving this vision. You must believe that you can alter your life by altering your attitude of yourself. What will it look and feel like when you achieve your vision? How will your life unfold differently as a result? If you can't visualize yourself achieving your vision, chances are you won't. Reimagine what your life will be.

Third, spend time writing out your vision. Break it down into different areas of your life. What is important to you? What makes you happy? How will you define success? Look to define your vision in all the areas of your life – personal, career, relationships, finances, education, spiritual and so on. Create clarity in each one.

Fourth, keep it visible. You must see your vision every day. Whether you write it in a journal, hang it on your refrigerator or put it on the mirror in your bathroom, it is imperative you keep your vision where you can see it often.

And finally, form a plan. Create clear action steps to move you closer to your vision. Think about what Lee Iacocca said, "The discipline of writing something down is the first step towards making it happen." Write down the plan and the action steps. By writing down the goal, plan and timeline, it sets in motion that which may never have happened otherwise. When you define your vision and consistently review it, you are, in reality, programming your thought processes to attract and create the experiences you consciously desire.

A fantastic resource to support this is a vision board. A vision board is a tool used to help clarify, concentrate and maintain focus on a specific vision. Literally, a vision board is any sort of board on which you display photos, drawings or words that represent whatever you want to be, do or have in your life. The idea behind this is that when you surround yourself with images of who you want to become, what you want to have, where you want to live, or even where you want to vacation, your life changes to match those images and those desires. The pictures and words add clarity to your goals and feelings to your vision itself.

There are different methods you can use to create your vision board. You can choose the one that works best for you. You don't need a lot to get started, just a piece of poster board, Bristol board or cardboard. You'll need a big stack of different magazines (or images from the Internet) and some glue or tape.

Getting started is simple. Get yourself into a creative environment, whether you need music or quiet, and then think of your desires and your vision. Get emotionally connected again. Now start flipping through the magazines or pictures that are in front of you and tear out the images and words that best reflect the vision or the desires that you have. Just make a big pile of them. Don't worry about gluing anything yet, just collect the ones that you need.

Once you've gone through all your magazines, then go through the images and begin to lay out the ones that are your favorites. Eliminate those images that no longer feel right for your vision. This is where your intuition comes into play. Lay the pictures that made the cut out on your board to get a sense of what you want. Your board could be centered on your career, education, health, or spiritual, emotional or personal aspects in your life, or it could be all of them together. Add writing if you want to. Paint on it. Add anything you need to make the board your reality. You could even leave space in the center of this vision board for a great photo of yourself in order to add motivation. A vision board is an incredible tool to motivate you visually every single day.

Consider this whole approach to visioning like you were the writer, director and actor in your own movie production. You're not only the actor, but the star of the movie. The scenes which are currently being played out, the experiences and outcomes of the events exist as a result of the script that you have previously written, or in many cases may have allowed others to write for you. You practice your script every day. If you don't like the reviews you're getting from your movie, rewrite a scene or two. If you don't like where the ending is heading, write yourself a happier one.

When you are in control of your success, you need to clearly define what that success means. When you define your vision, you are, in essence rewriting, or reimagining, the script and doing away with the scenes that you don't want to see and experience and replacing them with the scenes that you do. The result is a more enjoyable movie with some Oscar-winning scenes. It is your choice. Through consistency and daily review of the new script in the form of your written vision and vision board, the old script will quickly become overwritten and replaced with the scenes which you desire to see in the finished production.

In order for you to define your vision in a way that is effective, it is necessary to know it inside out in great detail. You must see it, feel it and embrace it. The vision needs to trigger and ignite strong positive emotions within you.

Define your vision and create a vision board that elicits deep feelings of fulfillment and a real sense of joy. Start attracting those positive things in your life by creating clarity in your desires and by believing in yourself.

And remember to always dream big. Michelangelo said, "I hope that I may always desire more than I can accomplish." I wish the same thing for you.

"Sometimes I lie awake at night, and I ask 'Where have I gone wrong?' Then a voice says to me,' This is going to take more than one night.' "
- Charlie Brown

CHAPTER FOUR: REclaim Control

"You are searching for the magic key that will unlock the door to the source of power, and yet you have the key in your own hands and you may use it the moment you learn to control your thoughts."
– Napoleon Hill

Napoleon Hill hit the nail right on the head. You already have control of your life. It's simply a matter of using it. What if I said you have much more control of your life than you think you do? The things that happen to you happen because of your own thoughts and your own actions. You have become exactly what you think you are. Does this mean you are supposed to blame yourself for everything that occurs in your life? No, not at all. It means you have to take responsibility for what happens in your life so you feel more in control and realize you are the one calling the shots.

Deepak Chopra said, "We think we live in the world, but the world lives in us." We all live in the same world, but the way we live is based on what we are taught. At any time in your life, you can choose to change who you are and how you act. If you want to renew yourself, you must take control of yourself. You have the potential, but you cannot simply stand around and wait, expecting great things to happen. You must take the first step.

A year ago, I lent my vehicle to Hannah, so Jane had to come and pick me up on her way home from work. We decided to go grocery shopping before going home; Lilly and Molly were all out of Dog Chow and we needed to pick up some odds and ends to get us to the end of the week.

When I got into the car, she said she was concerned by the loud noise it had been making on her way over. She said it would hesitate like it wanted to stall and then lurch forward, words you never want to hear when describing the performance of your car.

I dropped her off at the store and took the car for a quick spin to see if the noise would repeat itself. Sure enough, as I made my way through town, the car proceeded to clank, bang and then outright stall. When I restarted the engine and went to put it in gear, my worst fears were realized, the transmission was gone. Couldn't be simple, could it. No, it had to be the transmission. To add insult to injury, we were two months away from the car loan being paid off.

I now had some choices to make. Yes, the fact that the car broke down was out of my control, however, my reaction and decisions were mine. I didn't like the situation, not at all, but I was still in control. I could have a fit; curse and kick the tires. I could walk away and deal with it another day. I could go back to the grocery store and angrily ask my wife what she did to the car to make it break. Or I could get help. I called the automobile assistance program I'm a member of and they towed the car to the dealership where I bought it.

Now what? I had another decision to make at the dealership. I could storm into the building, saying I was a victim of shoddy workmanship. Would it make me feel better? Maybe. Would it solve my problem faster? Probably not. I needed to maintain control of my emotions. It was not the dealership's fault that my car broke down. I calmly explained the situation. I looked at my options and decided not to rush into a decision until I had all the facts. The dealership agreed and gave me a loaner car. They also offered to let me take home different vehicles each day in case I wanted to purchase another vehicle instead of fixing my broken one. All decisions well within my control.

Jane and I went home and laughed at the situation. Yes, we didn't like what happened, but it could have been worse. It was summer, not the middle of winter. We were getting groceries, not going to an event out of town. I chose not to let it ruin my evening with my family. I always had the choice to stay in control. Think of how different the outcome would have been if I had chosen to lose control at any point throughout the evening. I bet someone would have been kicking the dog at some time. There's a Chinese proverb that says, "You cannot prevent the birds of sorrow from flying over your head, but you can prevent them from building nests in your hair."

Realizing you are in control is a terrific confidence boost, as it should be. Just don't lose sight of reality. There are many things you can't control. You can't control the weather, decisions that were made in the past, the fact that there is only 24 hours in a day, the laws of nature, other people's thoughts, emotions and behaviors, and so forth. You can influence some of these things and possibly persuade others to go in the direction you want, but you can't control them. You just can't.

Stop trying to and start focusing on what you can control. This is one of the hardest concepts for many people to grasp, but once they do, it is liberating, rather than limiting. By accepting the fact that you don't have control over everything, you give yourself the opportunity and permission to forgive yourself for mistakes. Alternatively, you can make your best even better by working toward making better choices. It is like James Arthur Ray said, "Control is never achieved when sought after directly. It is the surprising outcome of letting go."

You only have control over one thing: you. You control your thoughts, your emotions and your behavior. You're at this point in your life because of all your decisions. Recognize that everything you do is based on choice. You always make a choice, even if you don't like any of the options. Choosing to do nothing is still making a choice. Choosing to walk away is a choice. Sticking it out, fighting back, taking charge, starting over, admitting defeat and declaring victory are all choices. It is your job to choose wisely.

Anthony Robbins said, in essence, that if we want to direct our lives, we must take control of our consistent actions. It's not what we do once in awhile that shapes our lives, but what we do consistently. To take control of our consistent actions means changing our thinking about which actions we have control over.

The power of RE is realized when you accept the fact that you are in control of yourself and you responsibly and deliberately exercise your right to choose.

I was fortunate enough to spend many years enjoying our family cottage at Kawagama Lake. Our cottage was on an island and I spent many weekends laughing, swimming, boating and just hanging out with my friends and family. Some of my most memorable experiences, and lessons, came not from when I was having fun, but from when I was *working* at the cottage.

The cottage was built from the ground up by my parents. They transformed it from a piece of land covered in trees to a beautiful family haven, complete with gardens, boathouse, two docks, and even an outhouse (our indoor plumbing came later). I learned a lot helping out over the years. The one time I remember vividly was when I helped build the boathouse as a teenager.

To build this boathouse, my father insisted we "do it right." Doing it right meant we had to dig a big hole starting from the shoreline. And when I say dig, I literally mean dig with a shovel, not a back hoe. This hole was 20 feet wide by 20 feet long and the back wall of the hole measured about 16 feet from the bottom to the top. It took three weeks of solid backbreaking work removing dirt, rocks and roots. This may sound strange, but it was a great three weeks working alongside my father. He taught me many things I still apply to my life today.

When we were digging this massive hole, we would unearth some big boulders. These rocks had to be moved. Now, being the young buck I was, I would try to use brute force. This amused my father to no end, but I insisted. As I heaved and sweated, he stood by and watched. I'm sure a time or two I heard him chuckling. When my body was finally worn out and my pride subdued, he taught me something important. He told me that even the biggest boulders can be moved easily if you choose to approach the situation properly. He showed me how to use steel bars to gain leverage off of smaller rocks to maneuver the bigger boulders out of the way.

Boulders are always cropping up in life, rising up as challenges or barriers to success. You can try and use brute force, exerting lots of effort and wearing yourself out or you can choose to look at the situation differently. Albert Einstein said that "We can't solve problems by using the same kind of thinking we used when we created them." You must change your thinking and change your approach to challenges that appear immovable. You must regain control.

The following are five questions that when answered in order will allow you to grab hold of the reins of your life. They are simple and can be applied to most any situation where you want to make an impact. You can positively influence your relationships, career, happiness and any other aspect of your life. To take greater control of your life, you have to honestly assess where you are currently.

Question One: What's your problem?

How often have I heard my teenagers say this to me? However, usually when they say it, it's accompanied by sarcastic undertones and a surly look. However, I want you to ask yourself this question in good faith. Be objective. By answering this question truthfully, you will give yourself a benchmark or foundation to gaining more control in your life. Are you a control freak? Do you see life as full of obstacles? Are you ticked off or negative all the time? Are you sad, depressed and complain a lot? This step is imperative. It requires confidence and courage to answer without lying. The time invested in answering will give you incredible value on your journey of growth. It is difficult to achieve results without identifying what your problem is. Take a good look in the mirror.

Question Two: How are your problems affecting your life?

This question helps you uncover and identify the impact of your thoughts and behaviors. To get control of your life, you must be responsible for what is happening in your life right now. Are you as good a parent, spouse, friend or dog owner as you could be? Are you a workaholic? Do you have bad habits that get in the way of your success? Does your tendency to procrastinate stall projects and activities? This question requires absolute self-honesty. As the saying goes, the truth will set you free.

Question Three: Where are your problems coming from?

You need to separate excuses from responsibility. Are your problems from external factors that are out of your control or are they germinating from within? External factors that you have no control over are where excuses breed. You can blame other people for your problems, you can play a victim to circumstances or environment, you can seek pity or attention because of a bad situation, but ultimately it is always your choice. Seek out and separate excuses from where your responsibility and influence truly reside. Look to your successes and accomplishments. Identify your strengths and priorities. Fuel your courage to take action in areas and tasks that are directly your responsibility. You will notice an immediate impact on the level of control in your life.

It's like Ralph Waldo Trine, philosopher, mystic, teacher and author of many books, said, "To get up each morning with the resolve to be happy is to set our own conditions to the events of each day. To do this is to condition circumstances instead of being conditioned by them."

Question Four: What do you want?

When I ask people this, many can't define what it is they want in their lives. They know what they don't want though. They spend so much energy complaining or obsessing about what they don't want or about the lack of control they have in their lives that they forget to ask themselves what they actually want their lives to look like. The problem exists when you spend so much time focusing on what's wrong in your life that you actually relinquish and end up getting stuck. When you can tell yourself specifically what you want, you will be well on your way to achieving your goals.

Until you can actually list your desires in order of their importance, you will be a victim to circumstance. It is through clarity of vision and goals and acquiring a true desire for what you really want that your mind can reprogram itself and you begin taking steps towards reaching your goals.

Question Five: What do you need to do to achieve this?

You now need to put actions to your goals. You can't just think your way into a new situation. You can't sit back and keep wishing and dreaming for things to be different. You must act on these thoughts. You need to break the habits that are currently holding you back and start forming new ones to move you in the direction of your desires. You must act your way into change. Action creates control. Write out your actions towards achieving your goals and then every day put one new action into play to meet them. These actions alone will bring greater control into your life.

You must act; however, you must act with the end in mind. What do you want to accomplish? What does success look like? Sometimes we are in such a hurry to change and add more excitement to our lives that we act with the best intentions, but don't think all the way through. This can create headaches. The path to hell is paved with good intentions.

For the most part, I was a pretty good kid, really. But all teenagers do some stupid things without thinking about the consequences. I'm sure it's in the handbook. Like the time I thought it would be fun to throw snowballs at buses, even though I was told by my parents not to. I figured, what could be the harm? What I didn't factor into my plan was my mother sitting on my target bus coming home from work and my snowball hitting the same window she was looking out of. Just my luck.

I wasn't alone in my pranks. I had some terrific friends growing up (don't worry guys, your names will be protected, especially yours Mike). On Thursday evenings, Girl Guide and Brownie meetings were held in our church basement. As young boys will, we liked to sneak into the basement and listen to what was being said. One night during the Christmas holidays, we hit a big break. The girls were planning to form a circle around two large trees in the middle of the parking lot near a strip mall and sing carols for passersby. Every year, these trees are decorated from top to bottom with large Christmas lights.

We devised what we thought was a brilliant plan. We ran over to the trees before the girls and climbed close to the top where we were completely hidden from view and waited patiently for the girls to arrive. We covered our mouths with our mitts to stifle our snickers when we heard them coming. As the troop started to sing, we gently unscrewed the large Christmas bulbs and tossed them from the top of the tree behind the girls to scare them. And it worked. Can you imagine the sound of six bulbs flying through the air at once and shattering on the pavement below? It sounded just like gunshots. The girls screamed and we high fived our success.

Then we discovered the hole in our plan when one of the leaders yelled, "Who's up there? Come down right now. I can wait all night." We hadn't thought that far ahead. The power and control had shifted from our tall perch to the ground.

I'm not saying I'm proud of what I did (however, I still chuckle when I think of those girls screaming), but in both cases I acted quickly without thinking what the end result would look like.

Why don't more people have more control of their lives? Because the majority of people are going around and around in a circle, like a dog chasing its tail, waiting. They run in loops watching life pass them by while they spend a lot of energy just getting dizzy. What are they waiting for? They're waiting for that day when life will just suddenly happen for them. They're waiting for someone to come along and solve their problems. They're waiting for something to fall out of the sky or for lightning to strike. They may not even be sure what that sudden lightning strike will contain, but they think they'll know it when they see it. They're going to be waiting for a long time. But they don't mind, because after a while the waiting becomes a habit which is now safe and comfortable. Their waiting habit confirms that it's not their fault and that their success is no longer within their control. Before they know it years have passed by and all they did was wait.

Or worse yet, someone else took control. This often happens to people who don't maintain control of their lives. They let someone else take over pull them along into something that they may not want: professionally, religiously or personally. Before they know it their head is shaved, they're sitting in a circle wearing a white robe and someone's handing them a cup of "freshie."

Don't let this be you. Remember these wise words said by Jack Welch, businessman, author and Chairman and CEO of General Electric from 1981 to 2001, "Control your own destiny or someone else will." There is so much more to life than this and you deserve so much more. You can make it all happen just by making the decision to take control of your life. Do it today. Decide that right this second things are going to change. You don't have any more time to waste.

Don't let your life end up like Mitch Robbins in the movie *City Slickers*. Mitch, played by Billy Crystal, lost control of his life and wasn't sure how to get it back. In front of a classroom of children during career day, his total lack of enthusiasm comes out in this speech:

> Value this time in your life kids, because this is the time in your life when you still have your choices, and it goes by so quickly. When you're a teenager you think you can do anything, and you do. Your twenties are a blur. Your thirties, you raise your family, you make a little money and you think to yourself, "What happened to my twenties?" Your forties, you grow a little pot belly, you grow another chin. The music starts to get too loud and one of your old girlfriends from high school becomes a grandmother. Your fifties you have a minor surgery. You'll call it a procedure, but it's a surgery. Your sixties you have a major surgery, the music is still too loud, but it doesn't matter because you can't hear it anyway. Seventies, you and the wife retire to Fort Lauderdale, you start eating dinner at two, lunch around ten, breakfast the night before. And you spend most of your time wandering around malls looking for the ultimate in soft yogurt and muttering "How come the kids don't call?" By your eighties you've had a major stroke and you end up babbling to some Jamaican nurse who your wife can't stand, but who you call "mama." Any questions?

Later in the movie, the tough, crusty old cowboy Curly tells Mitch what the real secret to living a life of no regrets is.

"Do you know what the secret of life is?" Curly said holding up one of his fingers, "This."

"Your finger?" Mitch said.

"One thing. Just one thing," Curly said, "You stick to that and the rest don't mean shit."

"Well, that's great," said Mitch, "But what's the 'one thing?'"

With a small smile, Curly said, "That's what *you* have to find out."

Spend time identifying what it is that you want. Those things that inspire you, excite you and make you want to jump out of bed in the morning. The things that bring you true happiness. Use these images to regain control of your life.

The one thing that stops most people from taking control of their lives is fear. Simply put, fear is an emotional response to a perceived threat. It is a basic survival mechanism which occurs in response to a specific stimulus, such as pain or the threat of danger. In our caveman ancestors, fear kept them from being eaten, today it keeps us from wandering down too many dark alleyways. However, often our fear holds us back from taking control off our lives and making changes. So many people are paralyzed because they are afraid of what will happen in the future, such as a situation getting worse or that something unacceptable will not be resolved. Other times, our fear is an immediate reaction to something happening in our present that stops us from moving forward, such as not wanting to interview for a new job because of a fear of failure.

Fearing the future is just silly. The future is always changing based on the decisions you are making today. As Gandhi said, "I do not want to foresee the future. I am concerned with taking care of the present. God has given me no control over the moment following." Take control of the moment you are given and the future will take care of itself.

As for fears that plague your present, it is helpful to understand that we develop fears as a result of learning and thus, we can unlearn them. In the field of psychology, this is known as fear conditioning. Some fears are good for our health and we should keep them. I would never suggest approaching a tiger in order to get over your fear of cats. However, a fear of public speaking could seriously delay your growth as a person. Seth Godin, author of the bestselling book *Linchpin* said, "Fearlessness does not mean without fear. It just means not fearing the things that you shouldn't be afraid of. There is a difference between being fearless and being reckless."

Once you are able to distinguish the difference between good for you fears and bad for you fears, you can work on unlearning the ones that are hindering you. You can retrain your brain to manage and reduce the fear.

What is the scariest thing you've ever done? Was it buying your first car? Or your first home? Was it the first day of your first job? Heading off to university? Asking someone to marry you? Rushing to the hospital the day your child was born? Maybe it was even further back, picking up your first date or going in for that first kiss. Remember all the anxiety and worry leading up to the big moment? Scary, right? But what a feeling! I bet you felt alive. I'd put money on it that as soon as you made the decision to just go for it and did it, that it felt like no big deal. You probably thought you'd wasted a lot of time worrying for nothing. Amelia Earnhardt once said,

> The most difficult thing is the decision to act, the rest is merely tenacity. The fears are paper tigers. You can do anything you decide to do. You can act to change and control your life; and the procedure, the process is its own reward.

You see, some fears may look like tigers, something to be feared and avoided, but they are in fact merely paper and easily overcome if you take action against them. Are you letting your fear of paper tigers hold you back?

As a child I don't remember having a lot of fear. I played sports, had a great circle of friends, did well in school and had a supportive home life. I do, however, remember the fear I felt when it was announced to my sixth grade class that we would be participating in a public speaking contest. I was so nervous preparing for that speech. I wrote out all my notes on those small three by five inch cards. I practiced over and over again. I remember standing in front of a mirror while my dog, Gussy, a big German Sheppard, lay on my bed watching attentively, like he understood every word I said.

All the while though, I could feel those paper tigers prowling around in my head, gnawing at my confidence, putting ideas in my mind. I was terrified to fail in front of everyone. I envisioned forgetting my speech, saying something stupid, throwing up or even fainting. Fortunately, I won my battle with my paper tigers. I walked up in front of everyone and gave it my best, despite the fact that my hands were shaking so badly I couldn't read the cards. Fortunately, with all my practice, I didn't need to. I delivered my first speech on the benefits of having a pet rock and I won the competition. I was ecstatic, exhausted and really proud of my 12 year old self. The paper tigers were gone, torn to bits.

This small action, rewarded with success, gave me the confidence to do it all over again in grade seven. Of course, being a year older, I felt that it was only fitting I choose a more serious topic. My grandfather had glaucoma, so I talked about that. I won that competition too. Little did I know that this would be the fledgling start of my career, speaking in front of groups consisting of anywhere from 15 to 2000 people. What if I had let the paper tigers paralyze me? What would I be doing now?

Paper tigers are a normal part of life. You learn from your experiences with them. These are the fears you will be facing when you decide to take control of your life. It may seem scary and overwhelming at first, but as soon as you make the decision to change and take that step forward, the fear will melt away and you'll realize you can do it.

Don't listen to words of doubt that may bounce around in your head as you act on your desire for more control. Thoughts of fear and doubt are just habits, but they are strong enough to hold you where you are right now if you let them. Remember, gaining more control in your life starts with your thoughts. Start thinking about what you stand to gain. Think about how you will feel when you have control of the life that you desire and focus on those positive thoughts. Once you have made the decision to step up to the plate and accept the challenge, then you will just naturally do whatever needs to be done.

Don't be afraid to see yourself achieving new heights. Dream big. Imagine yourself in complete control, doing what you want to do, feeling what you want to feel, eliminating worry and anxiety from your life. See it, feel it, believe it. Fear stops people dead in their tracks. They would rather play it safe and live well within their comfort zones than risk the possibility of trying something different and failing. But not you. You are not using phrases like "I don't deserve it" or "I can't do that" because you've replace them with "I do deserve good things in life" and "I can and will accomplish what I set my mind to do." You made the decision to break through fear and abolish comfort zones in order to move forward in a life full of self-control, confidence and fulfillment. You are now the author of your own reality. And there are no paper tigers in that reality.

You can achieve your goals simply by focusing on the big picture and only on the positive aspects of your journey towards it. You'll be amazed at what a difference it will make in your life simply by challenging your thoughts. You'll notice an increase in energy and a new zest for life. You'll wake up each day with a new bounce in your step simply because you made the decision to live life instead of waiting for it.

Remember the phrase "do-over?" When you were young and made a mistake or didn't perform well in a game or activity, it was just natural to ask for a do-over. It was right up there with "shot gun" and "jinx." I golf with friends who still use do-overs, they've just disguised them as "mulligans." If you have a bad shot, it doesn't count and you can shoot again. The only rule is one mulligan per nine holes of golf.

Unfortunately, the only people who get to use do-overs or mulligans are kids and golfers. There are no do-overs in life. I wish there were. All you can do is learn from situations and change what you can. But let's imagine for a moment that life did have do-overs. What if you were able to project yourself 20 years into the future and see all the events that impacted your life and you were given a single do-over. You would be able to change any of the events and situations that may have taken you off course.

While this is impossible, a clear vision will act in the same manner as a do-over. If you can see clearly now where you want to be, what you want to achieve and what kind of person you want to be, then there is less chance you will ever need a do-over. You will be able to confidently manage each day and make your vision a reality.

Oprah Winfrey (yes, I have watched a few episodes, now get off my back) said, "It isn't until you come to a spiritual understanding of who you are – not necessarily a religious feeling, but deep down, the spirit within – that you can begin to take control." If you figure out what you want yourself and your life to look like now, you will have more control over what happens to you because you will be able to make the decisions that will move you towards that vision. It's about having a purpose.

Let me illustrate what happens when you slacken your control on your life and who you want to be. There was once a mechanic who was ready to retire. He had spent his years rebuilding classic cars and was considered by many to be one of the best in the area. He told the shop owner of his plans to retire and spend more time with his wife and family. They'd been careful to save their money over the years (even when times were tough) and he was confident they'd be able to live a comfortable life off their nest egg. He loved working on the cars, especially the satisfaction he got taking them out for that first spin before their owners came for them. He'd have liked to work a few more years to save up money for his own, but his wife was right, he should enjoy the time he had left.

His boss was sad to see him go, but understood. He asked the man if he'd finish one last car that had been brought to the shop the other day. It was a 1967 black Chevy Impala with a V8 327 four barrel engine. The man agreed and spent the next few months restoring the car. However, his mind was no longer in his work and he didn't treat the car with the same meticulous care he was known for. It was a disappointing conclusion to all his years of hard work.

When he finished the car, he took it out for a spin. The engine didn't purr quite as nicely as usual and the ride wasn't as smooth as it could have been, but the man figured the car's owner wouldn't notice. Only someone with his years of experience would be bothered by the small things he'd missed.

When he returned to the shop, the man handed the keys to his boss. The boss shook his hand and thanked him for all his dedicated work. He said he hoped the owner of this car would appreciate all the time and effort the man had put into it.

The man agreed and started to walk away when his boss called out his name and tossed him the keys. "My gift to you," he said. The man stared at the keys in shock and then dismay. If only he had known he was working on his own car, he would have been so much more careful and attentive.

So it is with us. We build our lives in a distracted way, rather than acting thoughtfully, understanding that our actions affect our lives. We are willing to put up with less than the best. When it matters most, we sometimes don't give our best effort, then we are shocked to find that we are driving a car we have built with a misaligned tires, a an engine that stalls and no do-over to make it go away.

See yourself as the mechanic. Think about the car as you. It is the vehicle you take through life. Each day you tune the engine, align a tire or adjust the suspension. Maintain it wisely. You are all you'll ever have. Even if you live for only one more day, that day deserves to be lived graciously and with dignity. Your bumper sticker should say, "This life is a do-it-yourself project." Is there any clearer way to say it? Your life today is the result of your attitude and choices in the past. Your life tomorrow will be the result of your attitude and the choices you make today.

So what are you waiting for? Take control. Change your attitude. Burn up the paper tigers that are your fears. Take action. It's a decision away and it's waiting for you to take the first step. Do it today and you'll never look back. Everything you've ever wanted can be yours and all you have to do is change your thinking and reclaim control.

"I am not a has-been. I am a will be."
- Lauren Bacall

CHAPTER FIVE: REnew Your Confidence

Recently, I had a video crew come in to record a couple of my keynote speeches so we could edit them for use as short marketing clips. I have to admit, I loved it. I find it exhilarating and rewarding presenting to large crowds.

As our team discussed how we would edit them, one of my colleagues said, innocently, "What have you got to offer?" I didn't really understand the question at first and upon further discussion, the comment was pertaining to how to promote and position my presentations.

She went on to explain that her research into how others were marketed revolved around a great achievement or a major challenge they had overcome in their lives. There were gold medal athletes, people who had gone from rags to riches, some who had climbed Mount Everest and those with near death experiences. One man had even been born with no arms and was abandoned by his parents, but through the efforts and encouragement of his foster parents had learned to use his feet as his hands and gone on to be an award winning musician. I mean, this guy played the piano *and* drums in his presentations!

In light of all these great people, what *did* I have to offer? That question alone has derailed the confidence of many people. It becomes a question of self-worth. It forces you to reevaluate your confidence in yourself.

I know the question was related to marketing and promotion, but if I wasn't passionate and clear about what I set out to accomplish, I could have easily taken it to heart, panicked and questioned my efforts. I didn't because I am confident with who I am and what I do.

So, for the record, I have overcome some medical issues. I have had my heart broken and broken some hearts myself back in the day. I had a full head of hair and then lost it (I'm still looking for it). I had a stable family upbringing with great role models for parents. I am educated and have always had a job. I play sports, have been scuba diving and even flown a two-seater Zenair plane. I have owned or been part owner of four companies. I have had my struggles and challenges, but have also experienced many achievements and successes.

I have a great passion for life. I am like a large majority of the people I speak to, I'm like you. My life has value because of the way I choose to live it and how I choose to influence others because of it. There are many decisions I have made throughout my life to get me to where I am now. Some good, some bad, and they have all shaped the way I view the world now. I accept ownership of all of them.

Confidence comes from accepting responsibility for who you are today. Confidence comes from recognizing that you add value to your life and those people in your life. Confidence comes from defining an even better tomorrow and believing that you will achieve it. Confidence comes from accepting that you deserve to have more joy in your life and a willingness to go out and get it.

All this from one question: What have you got to offer? But this is the question that plagues so many of us. We doubt ourselves. What if you could just bury those things that are holding you back, the things that make you doubt yourself, the people who make you uncertain, the situations that make you hesitate? Would this give you a new lease on life?

The thing that always surprises me about people is that they don't believe they deserve the best out of their lives or they just plain don't believe in themselves. Here's a powerful thought for you: Other people's perceptions of you are directly impacted by your own perception of yourself. If you don't believe you deserve personal greatness, they won't believe you do either and they will treat you accordingly. However, if you believe in yourself, others will too. As Henry Ford said, "Whether you think you can or not – your right."

A lack of confidence often manifests itself as negativity. You may think you are confident, but if pesky negative thoughts are always creeping into your head, saying you might not be good enough or that you shouldn't try because you might fail, it's probably time to give your confidence a boost. It's not who you are as a person that is holding you back. It's who you think you are not. There are simple steps you can take to build up your confidence, and they are something everyone can do. The negativity will slowly fade away, and you will be able to see your goals and dreams more clearly.

In speaking with some of my past clients, I noticed a lot of them shared a similar problem It's called the "I can'ts." You know what I mean. "I can't possibly take the time to do that" or "I can't get up in front of a crowd and talk" or "I can't approach a stranger and say hello." Whenever I start hearing the "I can'ts," I love telling the story I read in *Chicken Soup for the Soul* called "The I Can't Funeral." The story was about a fourth grade teacher named Donna who wanted to teach her students to start thinking in terms of "I can" instead of "I can't."

So what did she do? She held a funeral. She asked her entire class to write down on a sheet of paper the words "I can't" in big letters and then make a list of all the things they couldn't do. As you can imagine, the lists covered all sorts of topics: from sports, to school, to friends. Donna even made her own list.

When all the lists were completed, the kids folded them in half and deposited them in a shoebox on her desk. With the box tucked under her arm, Donna led all the kids out of the classroom and to the yard. With a shovel she had grabbed from the custodian's room she dug a hole in the ground by the playground where she placed the box.

It was at this point that Donna delivered her eulogy and I think it is something that every person, young and old, can benefit from hearing. She said:

> Friends, we are gathered here today to honor the memory of I Can't. While he was with us on Earth, he touched the lives of everyone, some more than others. His name, unfortunately, has been spoken in every public building: schools, city halls, state capitols, and yes, even our White House. Today we have provided I Can't with a final resting place. He is survived by his brothers and sisters: I Can, I Will and I'm Going to Right Away. They are not as well known as their famous sibling and are not as strong and powerful… yet. Perhaps, someday with your help they will make an even bigger mark on the world. May I Can't rest in peace and may everyone present pick up their lives and move forward in his absence. Amen.

Donna created a paper tombstone for I Can't that hung in the classroom for the rest of the year. Whenever one of the students would forget and say, "I can't..." Donna would point to the tombstone posted on the wall. More often than not, the student would revise their answer.

Just think how much people could accomplish if they'd hold a mental funeral for all their "I can'ts." What about you? What if you held one? It is time to for you to start believing that you can and that you do deserve all the best life holds for you. As Dr. Suess, that famous author who has been inspiring children to reach their dreams for years wrote:

You have brains in your head.
You have feet in your shoes.
You can steer yourself in any direction you choose.
You're on your own.
And you know what you know.
You are the guy who'll decide where to go.

I want you to start thinking like the guy (or gal) who'll decide where to go. Right now get out a few pieces of paper. On one sheet, write down the ten best things you've accomplished in your life. Maybe it's graduating from college, getting married, getting a promotion, the birth of your child or an award you won. Perhaps it was overcoming a challenge or hurdle.

On another page, take a few minutes and write down all your personal strengths. Everyone has different strengths, so don't be afraid to put down anything you want. They could be a good sense of humor, great listening skills, self-leadership, dedication, loyalty and so on. They can be personal or work-related, both are good. If you have friends and family that you know are willing to help you improve, ask them to add to your list.

On the last sheet of paper, put a line down the middle. On one side, write out what you perceive to be your weaknesses. On the other side, write down the actions you need to take to change them. A weakness is only a weakness if you let it be one. Go through your list and pick out the one that would make the biggest difference in your life if it were to change and start there. Look at your accomplishments, how did you get to them? Can you use the same strategies to overcome the weakness? Do the same with your strengths. What strengths can you use to change your weakness into a strength. For example, if you fear public speaking, but have a great sense of humor; why not try a night of standup comedy? If you fear meeting new people, but have good rhythm, take a dance class where you can let your moves do the speaking for you.

Keep all these pages in a place where you can look at them on a weekly basis and remind yourself of the good you've done and the good you have in you.

When my son was younger, I got involved in coaching his sports teams. I was lucky enough to coach while he was playing both baseball and lacrosse. It's very rewarding coaching a sports team for young people and I recommend that every adult should get involved doing something involving kids, whether it is coaching a sports team or being a leader for Boy Scouts or Girl Guides, just get involved. The reward comes when you know you played a part in opening up possibilities for a young person.

Confidence plays a major role in how much children enjoy activities like these. I discovered that I could tell when a young lad was approaching the plate whether he would hit the ball or swing out. It was in his body language walking up, the way he held his bat or dipped his helmet as he set up his stance. Those that lacked confidence in their ability were so convinced that they couldn't hit that it showed in their walk, their grip on the bat, their body positioning, but what bothered me the most was that it dampened their enthusiasm and enjoyment for the game. They were not having fun because they were self-conscious about performing badly in front of their family and friends.

This is the challenge of the good coach: how to influence thoughts and change emotions to positively impact the experience. I believe, more often than not, it's about self-expectations. The blossoming baseball player, even at a young age, wants and expects to be able to hit a home run. They know players who can do this get all the accolades. The beginner wants this, so as they approach the plate they picture themselves doing it. The problem, quite frankly, is that most kids just don't have the power initially (or ever) to hit the big one. The more they come up to the plate with this goal in mind and don't achieve it, the lower their confidence. It doesn't matter if they hit a good grounder or a double, they don't feel good about their abilities. The more they feel they have to meet these expectations, the lower their confidence gets and soon they're not able to hit anything. It becomes all or nothing.

My job as a coach was to shift expectations in order to build confidence by showing them that the other things they were good at were just as important as hitting a home run; a bunt down third line and placing singles over in right field were just as vital to the game as rounding all the bases in one go. We would practice these until their confidence grew. As their confidence increased, so did their enjoyment of the game and their self-worth and importance as part of the team. Now that they had confidence in themselves, I could work on developing other aspects of their game because their attitude had shifted from "I can't" to "I can."

I want you to start being aware of your confidence and how it changes throughout the day. Your goal is to attempt to find any patterns that exist. For instance, are there certain times of the day when you are not as confident as you could be? Are there certain situations when you feel unsure of yourself? Are there people in your life who cause you to get apprehensive when you are around them? Train yourself to watch for these situations. Then, when you have the patterns identified, work on solutions to make them better. Try to understand why the anxiety happens or what causes you to doubt yourself. By becoming aware of the stressors, you can work on solutions for overcoming them as well as mentally preparing yourself for when you are going to face them again.

For instance, if you know that being around a certain person makes you feel unsure of yourself, get to the root of the problem. Are you afraid you will make a mistake when you're talking to them? Are you concerned about their opinion of you? Remember, no one is perfect. It's important that you do not compare yourself to others. Others do not make you feel inferior, you make yourself feel inferior. You are not inferior, you are not superior. You are just *you*.

One of my colleagues told me a story once about a professor she had in university that has always stuck with me. She said that when she finds herself overwhelmed by other people, she remembers what he used to say and it brings her back to sitting in a lecture hall as a freshman when her whole life was ahead of her. The professor said, "No one else knows any more about the meaning of life than you do." Whenever she feels small compared to someone else, she thinks of this and it reminds her that she knows just as much as anyone else about the most important thing in life. At that point, what else matters? Does the fact that the other person has more education, a bigger vocabulary, better clothes, or higher title matter? No, not at all.

Fear of failure is another key reason that many people lack confidence. They are afraid to speak up or try something because they are concerned that if they do, they might be rejected or it might not work. There is nothing wrong with failing provided that you learn from it and continue to try. Often, what appears to be a failure at first, actually works out for the best in the future because you grow from the experience. This is called failing forward. Let your mistake be a stepping stone to finding a better you.

When you do make a mistake, take responsibility for it. Take ownership of what happened and work to make it better next time. Mary Pickford once said, "If you have made mistakes there's always another chance for you. You may have a fresh start at any moment you choose for this thing we call 'failure' is not falling down but staying down."

Imagine an animator who wanted to start his own business. He was turned down by dozens of banks, filed bankruptcy several times and was fired from his job because he lacked ideas. One editor told him that, by the look of his sketches, he had no talent. He ended up working out of a church basement infested with mice. If he lacked confidence in himself and his skills and quit because he was afraid to fail, he never would have sketched one of those mice and we never would have known Walt Disney and Mickey Mouse.

If a young boy, who after being cut from his high school basketball team went home and cried in his room, had decided to quit instead of practicing more and improving on his weaknesses, kids everywhere would never have laced up their Air Jordans and dreamed of being the next basketball superstar.

I can provide you with dozens of more examples: Beethoven was told he was a hopeless composer. Thomas Edison was told he was too stupid to learn. Winston Churchill was told he showed a lack of success. Wayne Gretzky was told he was too small and slow for the NHL. Yes, these are names almost everyone knows; however, before they were famous, they were just normal people, no greater than anyone else. They just had the confidence to rise above their challenges, harness their talents and not let anyone stop them.

You cannot allow yourself to be limited by the myth that you are average and not capable of succeeding and achieving great things. In fact, think of every single challenge and bad situation you have dealt with in your life. They are no longer here, but you still are because you have a special power in you. Who you think you are and who you have been conditioned to believe you are do not necessarily equal who you truly are. You are a wonderful, unique person with talents no one else has. It is your duty to stand up confidently and share them with the world. Oliver Wendall Holmes said, "What lies before us and what lies behind us are tiny matters compared to what lies within us."

The Pursuit of Happyness is a truly inspirational movie about how believing in yourself and having the confidence to go after your dreams can change your life. It is based on the true story of a man named Chris Gardner who was forced to live on the streets with his son after his wife left him while he took on an internship as a stockbroker in order to create a better life for the both of them. Chris maintained his determination as he faced trying to care for his son, make money so they could survive and put in the grueling hours necessary to fight for one paid position amongst 20 other candidates.

He knew there was a better way of life out there for them.

At one point in the film Chris, played by Will Smith, tells his son, "You got a dream... You gotta protect it. People can't do somethin' themselves, they wanna tell you you can't do it. If you want somethin', go get it. Period." This is how you should view your own life. There are always going to be obstacles, challenges and barriers that are keeping you from the life you want, but you can't let them stop you. If you do, you will always be wondering what might have been and that's no way to live when you only get one chance.

While there is no quick fix for a lack of confidence, there are several things you can do to build it up over time. As you improve on the weaknesses you outlined earlier, you can also begin working on little things in your day-to-day life. If you continually do these things, you will create the positive habits that will set you on the road to improved confidence.

Look for the Good in Other People

Make an active effort to look for the good in other people and tell them. By looking for the best in others, you will also start to find the best in yourself. When you show other people the good in themselves, often these people will go out of their way to bring out your own strengths. By creating this type of positive environment, your confidence will grow.

Put it this way, have you ever had someone come up to you and give you a compliment on your hair or your clothes? You feel good about yourself, right? Now, do you ever find yourself looking at that other person a little more closely in order to try and repay the compliment? This is what looking for the good in others will do for you. People will start to look more closely at you and your unique talents and skills.

Learn to Accept Praise

I can't tell you how often I hear people receive a compliment and instead of just accepting it, they pass it off, make light of it or become embarrassed. Are you guilty of this? Most of us are. If someone sees fit to compliment you, by all means, take it. Accept compliments gracefully by looking people in the eye, smiling and saying, "Thank you."

Believe that you deserve the compliments you receive. Other people would not have given them if they didn't think you merited them. The more you can internalize the good things people say about you, the more you will start to accept them as true and your confidence will grow. A little praise is good for you as long as you as you don't go out of your way searching for it.

Practice

Practice things you are uncomfortable with. If you have trouble speaking with other people or entering a room full of people, start taking small steps. Begin by saying hello to people more often or making eye contact. You don't have to strike up a whole conversation, just give them a smile, look them in the eyes and say hi. If you're going into a room where you don't know anyone, visualize ahead of time that everyone there is your friend, you just haven't met them yet. Confidence isn't innate, it is a skill and like every other skill, the more you participate in situations that require confidence and the more you practice, the more confident you will be.

One of my co-workers likes to tell the story about her mom going away to college. Her mom had very low self-esteem and confidence. However, she still chose to go to a large school in Toronto over four hours away from home. She came from a tiny town with only 305 people (seriously, that's what it says on the sign), where everyone had known one another since kindergarten, so this new environment was overwhelming to say the least.

For the first few weeks she couldn't bring herself to go to the cafeteria because she thought everyone was looking at her. That's right, as she entered, she said she felt as if everyone turned and stared at her as she walked through, watching. She was so self-conscious of making a mistake and having everyone laugh at her that she just stopped going. Let's just say that this is one way to lose weight. Don't let a lack of confidence starve you of the richness life has to offer.

Surround Yourself with Positive People

Do any of the people in your life make you feel like you are less than you really are? Do they drag you down and make it difficult to keep a positive attitude? Remember, a lack of confidence manifests itself in negativity. You need to be positive to be confident and that requires the people you spend the most time with to be positive as well. After all, attitudes are contagious. Minimize your time with negative people as much as possible. When you're around them, avoid getting drawn into gossip or speaking negatively about situations or other people. Try to change the topic for the better or excuse yourself at the earliest chance. If someone does try to bring you down personally or insults you, take it with a grain of salt and remind yourself that no one is perfect, including them. David Brinkley said that "A successful person is one who can lay a firm foundation with the bricks that others throw at him or her." Do this and you won't crack under the pressure of negativity.

French daredevil Jean-Francois Gravelet is an excellent example of what increased confidence can do for you. Under the stage name Charles Blondin, he gained worldwide fame as the first person to walk across the Niagara Falls on a tightrope. He didn't stop there though, to the delight of amazed fans, he continued to come up with even more daring feats. He crossed the falls blindfolded and backwards. He would stop and lie down on the tightrope as if sleeping or take pictures of the crowds below. One time he took a chair out, balanced it on the wire and stood upon it. Another time, he carried out a stove and cooked an omelet and then ate it, all on the wire!

The Buffalo *Repulic* describes what it was like to be in the crowd during these acts in an article dated July 15th, 1859:

> He mounts the rope – in his hands rests the pole and a hat – he faces his auditory on the American side, and crosses the chasm backwards – he pauses in his career – he lays down upon the rope – he rises gently from his position as a wearied soldier with his martial cloak around him, and proceeds on his journey confident of the victory. Every heart beats with fear as he proceeds backwards up the slack fastened to the Canadian shore. Undaunted he moves along over the yawning abyss, until his foot once more touches *terra firma*. Here, where once was heard no sound save the war-whoop of the savage, ascends cheer after cheer

from the assembled throng, the belching of the locomotives, and music from the band.

Blondin is most often remembered for one particular bold exploit in which he steered a wheelbarrow across the chasm. The crowd held its breath as dangerous step after step he moved across the wire. Upon reaching the other side, it was said that the cheers of the crowd were louder than the roar of the falls. At this point, Blondin stopped and faced the crowd.

"Do you believe I can carry a person across in this wheelbarrow?" he asked.

Of course, the crowd shouted "Yes!" One gentleman, caught up in the enthusiasm of the moment, came up to him and said, "You are the greatest tightrope walker in the world. You can do anything!"

"Okay," said Blondin to the man, "Get in the wheelbarrow."

The story goes that neither the man, nor any of the crowd who moments ago believed he could do anything were willing to put him to the test. Having confidence does not simply mean having confidence in yourself, it also means having confidence in those you believe in. When you commit to someone or something in your life, be sure you commit to it 100%. By showing confidence in other people, they will in turn show confidence in you, boosting your self-esteem.

Oh, and just so you know, in August 1859, Blondin's manager, Harry Colcord, did ride on Blondin's back across the falls.

Be Nice to Yourself

Another crucial habit you need to adopt is a more forgiving internal dialogue. You wouldn't believe the number of people I've coached who tell me they want to improve their confidence and yet continue to tell themselves they can't do things. If you believe you can, you can. If you believe you can't, you can't. Telling yourself you can't do something will do you no good. You need to do whatever it takes to make yourself believe you can do it. American crime novelist, Roberick Thorp, wrote in his novel, *Rainbow Drive*, that "We have to learn to be our own best friends because we fall too easily into the trap of being our own worst enemies."

Writers, artists, actors and others in creative fields are often known for thinking their work and thus themselves aren't good enough. In his novel, *Teach Yourself: Writing a Novel and Getting Published*, Nigel Watts writes, "If there was somebody else with exactly the same qualities as yourself, would you dismiss them thus? If not, what gives you the right to judge yourself by a different criteria?"

Replace your internal bad mouthing with more positive self-talk. Ralph Martson had a great list of words you should stop using in your day-to-day life, both internally and externally. Try to make a point of dropping them from your vocabulary whenever possible. He said the words were:

• But	• Would have
• Try	• Could have
• If	• Can't
• Might	• Don't

You might wonder why it is so important to avoid these words. Let's review what they actually do to your way of thinking and that of those around you when you use them. When you use the word "but," it negates any thoughts or words that were stated before it because all you remember is what comes after the words.

Remember what Yoda in *Star Wars* said about the word "try"? He said there is either do or not do. There is no try. The minute you say try, you are already assuming there's some level of failure.

The word "if" suggests doubt. "Might" does nothing definite; it leaves options. When you look at "would have," "should have" and "could have," all of them are empty promises. The words "can't" and "don't" force the listener to focus on the opposite of what you want.

These are classic mistakes that parents and coaches often make without knowing the damage of their error and something most people do to themselves every day. Reinforce the positive, not the negative. Focus on what you can do. Change your words to reflect this.

Confidence is mind over matter. You spend every day of your life from your first breath accumulating the knowledge, tools and experience to tackle challenges, solve problems and take advantage of opportunities that appear each day in your life. Don't let a fleeting moment of fear or doubt talk you out of taking action.

I remember vividly encountering my own moments of truth as a young lad at our family cottage. Like most kids, I learned how to swim in the shallow water by the shore. It was a big deal for me the first time I put my hands over my head, bent my knees and had the courage to dive (well, flop) into the water from the middle of the dock where the water was just deep enough, but not too deep. Although I could swim well, my confidence in my ability to keep myself afloat in deep water was low.

My mother was my cheerleader, as most moms are. While she encouraged me, my father, much more practical, took a different approach. Not heeding my cries that I wasn't ready to dive into the deep water, he marched me towards the end of the dock. Now, common sense says if you can swim in four feet of water, you can swim in 40 feet, but to me, it seemed unfathomable, but with a giant push (probably more like a little nudge, but fear has a tendency to exaggerate things), I was "helped" off the dock and into the water. And surprise... I could swim. I always had the ability to swim in the deep water; I was just listening to the wrong voice in my head. I spent the rest of the summer happily jumping, diving and doing cannonballs off the dock.

The next summer when we returned in the spring, my brothers and I raced down to the dock excited about the first swim of the year. I charged down the steps and onto the dock, my little feet scurrying to keep up until BAM, I was stopped in my tracks at the end of the dock as my brothers leapt off. Once again, I saw the bottomless water below. I had gotten used to it last summer, but the time away had lowered my confidence again. That little voice crept into my head again telling me I couldn't do it.

My parents, moving at a much more leisurely pace than us kids, found me at the end of the dock watching my brothers splash in the water below. My mother, assuming her role as my supporter, encouragingly told me that I could do it. My father, seeing that my mother's words weren't having the desired effect, strolled over, picked me up, carried me to the end of the dock and launched me into the water.

Both my parents knew I could swim; they just went about encouraging me in different ways. I needed both of them. I needed my mom with her kind words and my dad with his "take the leap" attitude. If my dad had just thrown me in the water without my mom's encouraging words, I probably would have panicked. Without my dad to give me the push, literally, that I needed, my mother's words wouldn't have been enough. This is the balanced approach you need to take when building your confidence. You need to encourage yourself with positive self-talk and you need to be able to jump. Confidence comes from doing. Once you've done it, you must encourage yourself with positive affirmations and keep doing it.

There were times in early spring when me, my brothers and friends would crowd around the dock daring each other to jump in the water that still held the icy chill of winter even though it was warm enough to dress in shorts and t-shirts. When no one was brave enough to jump in we would make an agreement that we would all jump in together at the same time.

I'm sure you've been in situations like this before. You start to wonder if everyone else is going to jump or are they going to chicken out and when your head clears the surface you'll find them laughing at you. What happens? Have you ever been the only one not able to take the leap and found yourself standing alone wishing you had jumped too?

Don't let your confidence become tainted and compromised by thoughts of what other people are going to do. The only way to win at the Jump off the Dock game is to make the decision that you are going to jump no matter what the others are going to do. If you end up being the only one in the water, that just means you were the only one brave enough to take the leap.

To renew your confidence, spend time identifying what you want to do… and jump. Don't base your own decisions on what others might think of you. What will you think of yourself if you don't do it? Take the leap and spend the time after acknowledging your success.

"Energy and persistence conquer all things."
- Benjamin Franklin

CHAPTER SIX: REenergize Yourself

If you're lucky, you will have special people enter your life that will add a new perspective to your own existence. These people will help you to look at life in new ways and appreciate it that much more. At this stage in my own life, I am fortunate to have several such people. Kim is one of them. She is the National Director of one of my clients I met her a few years back and she is one of the most gracious people I know. I truly admire the way she chooses to live life. The other day I received an e-mail from her in response to one I'd sent asking her how things were going. Her reply had a profound impact on me and I'd like to share it with you. She wrote:

> The last four weeks have been filled with 'life'... too much to even begin to capture in a few short lines... wonderful gatherings with family and friend gatherings at both our west coast and Quebec homes, meaningful work, the heartbreaking loss of a dear friend, followed the same day by the unexpected loss of a dear Uncle, new beginnings and profound

endings... as I said 'life.' I have always said that I want to live to be one hundred... simply because there is so much I want to do, see and experience. I have come to understand that the rent for a long life is that you will experience more joy... and also more sorrow. I will take them both.

Reenergizing yourself starts with embracing life. Understanding that life has its ups and downs, but it is always your choice how you want to face them.

I was standing on my deck the other day thinking about this when I was pleasantly distracted by the giggles and screams of my eight year old neighbor. His mom had set up a slip and slide and he was having a riot. You remember slip and slides? A sheet of plastic you roll out across the lawn, preferably down a hill, and you put the sprinkler over it to get it nice and wet and then take a running start and throw yourself onto it.

Well, this one was the Spiderman edition and mom was trying to get it just right. I could see her fussing, trying to get the water to spray on it perfectly in order to maximize her son's fun. I'm sure there was a picture on the box that showed the water spraying a certain way and kids sliding all the way to the end of it and she pictured her child doing the same thing. A Hallmark moment.

What I saw, however, was the little munchkin running full out and then with all his might diving onto the slide with his little surfboard and gliding about a quarter of the way and stopping right under the "spidey" hands. Not exactly the way mom envisioned, but he was having a ball because he didn't have any preconditioned notion of what should be happening. All he knew was that he was having a great time. His laugh was telling the story.

We all have preconceived ideas of what life should be all about, but it doesn't always turn out the way we planned. Wouldn't it be incredible if we chose to see life the way my little buddy does? Full of zest and energy? Enjoying and making the most of what we have?

Children and animals have no preconceived notions and that is one reason they are able to stay so energized. For example, to an adult, the only thing a box is good for is putting things into it. This is what we've been told, this is what we believe. For a child, a box is more than just a transport system. It can be a house, a race car or spaceship. A child can think of hundreds of things a box can be. In your mind, your couch is for sitting on and your table is for eating. But for your dog, the couch is a giant chew toy and the table is for lying down on when you are out of the house.

You need to start looking at things differently. Open your mind and you will find a whole new world where you can fully embrace the person you want to be, someone who loves life. When was the last time you rode with your head out the window? Try it sometime and you will find out just why your dog looks so happy and unhindered.

The first rule to reenergizing your life is to envision it being full of joy, excitement and possibilities. Each day may not always be great, but there is greatness in every day. If you have difficulty finding it, try looking at each day through the eyes of a child or your dog.

I wonder sometimes where along the way the sparkle of excitement and wonderment got snuffed out for some adults. I know people who struggle with excitement every day. What taints their view of the world? We are all born with the capability to find joy and happiness in our lives, but somewhere along the way, some people forget.

Christmas is always an exciting season for me. I love the family time, people wishing each other a happy holiday and watching the excitement on people's faces on Christmas morning.

As a child, I remember staring out the window with my brothers on Christmas Eve trying to catch a glimpse of Rudolph's red nose in the night sky. Usually sleep would overcome us and we'd head off to bed to dream about the next day without seeing anything. But every once in a while we'd be lucky enough to mistaken the light of an airplane for the trademark red beacon of Santa's sled and would rush back to our beds so we were not caught awake when old St. Nick arrived. Morning never came fast enough back then. By six we couldn't wait any longer and were begging our parents to let us into the living room to see if Santa had come.

When the Santa torch was passed on to me when I had children, I got to enjoy the tradition on a whole new level. I took new pleasure in the delight I saw in their eyes. Instead of cookies and milk, my kids put out Coke and dry sausages for Santa and hung carrots on the trees outside our house for the reindeer. When Evan and Hannah fell asleep, Jane and I would drink the milk, eat the sausages (my treat) and then go outside and stomp around in the snow and munch a few of the carrots.

There were a couple of years when we'd fall asleep with the intent of waking later and going out, only to find ourselves rushing around in the wee hours of the morning, drinking warm milk, eating dried out sausages (if the dogs hadn't gotten to them already) and scurrying around outside. I'm sure my neighbors found their own enjoyment in watching us.

Looking back on it, I wouldn't change it for the world. To really enjoy life, you need to change the lens you use to view it. You need to view the world anew with the excitement and wonder of a child. This type of life is not handed to you in a basket; it is something you must unearth from within.

The second rule to reenergizing your life is to keep things fresh and new. In my book, *The Orange Popsicle*, I talk about finding more enjoyment in life by breaking routine. I can't stress this point enough. You lose energy through routines. You reenergize when things are novel.

We've all heard of the terrible twos. That year (or in some cases, years) when nothing seems to please a child and they will throw a fit when even the smallest thing doesn't go their way. If you have kids, you know what I'm talking about. And if you're reading this book, you survived. Congratulations.

The terrible twos are usually looked at in a negative light; however, I think this time in a child's life is when they are learning how to fully embrace life and live it to its full potential. Prior to age two, a child's world is pretty limited to what's near the floor. Between crawling and learning to walk, a child's mini world encompasses everything that's beneath the kitchen table. Parents can easily child-proof this area, putting covers on electrical sockets, keeping cupboards locked and small objects off the floor.

However, when a child reaches the age of about two, their view of the world begins to change. They've reached a height whereby they can now see what's on and above the table. A whole new exciting world to explore. The parents now have a much harder time keeping the child safe. Little hands can now reach the top of the desk where the pens sit. They can grab the edge of plates on the table. They can pull lamps off of shelves. Now the parents have to say "no" to the child much more.

Before, when the parents were able to limit the child's world by keeping things out of reach, the child was unaware of the limits being imposed, now they know there is a whole big world out there and they are being prevented from exploring it to their fullest capabilities. The parents put boundaries on their happiness and this causes them to get frustrated and throw the dreaded tantrum. They want to see and do it all and due to safety and social restraints, they are being limited.

As adults, we are now capable of doing and seeing everything that we want to (within a few time, financial and health and safety boundaries), but we put self-imposed limitations on ourselves. We fall into the routine of living within a set of perceived boundaries and never realize that all we need to do is take ourselves to the margins now and then to reenergize ourselves.

I advocate that you start throwing some tantrums, internal ones that is. Start challenging the limits you've placed on yourself. Believe you don't have any rhythm? Sign up for a dance class. Are you always saying you can't cook? Invite people over for a fancy dinner party. Never thought you could stand up in front of a crowd and give a speech? Take public speaking lessons. Life is bigger than the playpen you've set up for yourself. Routine and living within a safe comfort zone won't cause you much stress, but they won't bring you much excitement either. You need to start stretching the boundaries you've created for yourself. Feeling alive is fuelled by change. You have the choice to make these changes.

This leads us to the third rule to reenergizing your life, which is to always remember that the person you are and the life you live is because of the choices you are making. I'm signed up to receive notes from Seth Godin's blog. If you've never heard of Seth before, he is a bestselling author of 12 books, entrepreneur and agent of change. While he specializes in marketing, he also provides excellent advice on living life in general. The other day I received a blog post entitled "The places you go." Seth writes about how inside us we have "rooms" that we go to where we know we will be in different states of being and feel different emotions. We have rooms to be more productive, to feel contentment or to sit in sadness or be filled with anxiety, joy or frustration.

The thing about these rooms that Seth stresses is that it is always your choice as to which room you spend your time in. If you spend most of your days at work frustrated, it is because you are choosing to be frustrated rather than finding a way out of that state of being. Granted, sometimes it does feel good to let off some steam, but when you are doing it all the time, it can turn you into a person that is angry at the world. When things get to be too much, it is okay to break down now and then, but when you get to the point where if one thing doesn't go your way the world comes crashing down, then life becomes a chore. It is you who makes the decision to spend time being sad or worried or angry.

Seth says you have an addiction when you are constantly going back to a room that is not good for you. This is similar to the gratification bounces I talked about at the beginning of this book. You do things that make you feel good for the short term, but are detrimental to you overtime. The choice is always yours to get up from the room, walk out the door and close it behind you. You need to start making choices to live in the places that are good for you and help you become the person you want to be. Each day, ask yourself if you are entering the rooms that will allow you to live your life to the fullest. Are these the rooms that excite you and give you energy? Lock all the others.

You need to find the things in life that you are passionate about. Choose to spend your energy on these things. Oprah Winfrey said, "Passion is energy. Feel the power that comes from focusing on what excites you." Your passion could be your work, your family, a hobby, whatever stimulates you and takes you into a room that makes you feel alive. While it may not be possible to stay in this room all the time, spend as much time as you can there.

Sarah Bernhardt or "Divine Sarah," arguably one of the most famous actresses of the 19th century said, "Life begets life. Energy creates energy. It is by spending oneself that one becomes rich." Bernhardt's passion was acting. Her whole life was focused on her craft. For a period of time she even slept in a coffin in order to help her better understand the many tragic roles she played. Her passion gave her the energy to continue her career even after her leg was amputated below the knee due to an injury she acquired jumping off a parapet during a show. She was confined to a wheelchair, but it didn't stop her from starring in productions.

Passion is all about not giving up easily. Passion isn't the fast-burning splendor of a child's sparkler that delights but for a minute. It is a glowing coal that continues to emit heat long after the fire has gone out. Passion requires you to give your energy. When you are committed to a dream and are willing to give it all you have, you will be amazed at the energy and excitement you get in return. Most people give up on themselves far too quickly. They encounter an obstacle and it stops them dead. They are unwilling to let go of their energy to overcome it.

Bottling up your energy does you no good. Energy left unspent will only leave you feeling unfulfilled and discontented with your life. You don't need to "save" your energy. You don't have a limited reserve of energy. As long as you are using it towards things that excite, stimulate and enliven you, you will produce more. William James said, "Most people never run far enough on their first wind to find out they've got a second. Give your dreams all you've got and you'll be amazed at the energy that comes to you."

Wouldn't it be nice to just flip a switch and turn into the Energizer Bunny? While it isn't quite as easy as flipping a light switch, you can flip a switch to get more energy into your life. It is an internal emotional switch. It is making the decision to be more energized and start the momentum.

To reenergize is all about momentum. Making the decision, to generate more energy and more excitement in your life is the first step. After that you need to take action to keep the ball rolling. There are many people that come home and sit on the couch unhappily for hours thinking about all the things they could be and all that they could accomplish. It is their own lack of action that forms a black hole, sucking the energy right out of them. Don't let this be you. If you're tired of not having any energy or stimulation in your life and are prepared to flip that switch, you must also be prepared to put action to those thoughts.

Have you ever not felt like going to the gym for a workout, but went anyway? While your workout started out slow, you quickly noticed how when the endorphins kicked in, so did your energy. Or how about waking up on a Saturday morning, still tired from a long week at work and the thought of a day of yard work ahead of you? After your breakfast, you begrudgingly put on your boots and headed out to the yard. Ever notice that it only takes a few minutes of actually doing the task and accomplishing something until your energy levels begin to pick up?

The word energy is derived from the Greek words "energeia" meaning "activity, operation" and "energos" meaning "active, working." Both of these words describe action. You cannot think your way into a life with more energy. You must act your way into it.

Energy has the amazing capability to be transferred. At the beginning of this book, I highlighted how negative energy could be passed from person to person in a family until the dog took the brunt of it. Fortunately, positive energy can also be transmitted between people. I bet you have people in your life that always leave you feeling energized just by talking to them. According to the Law of Attraction, we are always sending out either positive or negative energy. Therefore, we are always influencing others and being influenced by others in return. How you influence and are influenced is your choice.

It's like a magnet. If you rub a magnet with a metal rod, the rod will gain some of the characteristics of the magnet, acquiring its magnetic power. The same can be said about how you are affected by the people in your life. They can be supportive and pick you up when you are depressed or choose to stomp on you and keep you down with a few kicks (figuratively, that is). They can celebrate your accomplishments or downplay them because of their own outlook on life. How do you feel in both cases?

If you want more energy in your life, you must surround yourself with more energetic people and put yourself into situations and events that are full of liveliness. You must also have the courage to limit contact with, or remove yourself completely, from other people's negative sphere of influence.

As parents we don't want our children playing in a puddle of dirty water with their best Sunday outfit on because we know it is impossible for them to play in that puddle and not get a speck of dirt on them. The only way to avoid the dirt is to refuse access to it in the first place. If you don't want dirt or negativity in your life, you must refuse to play in those puddles.

I'm not saying that you should automatically judge all those around you as a positive or negative influence right off the bat. Yes, there will always be people who are perpetually negative and you should stay away from them because they will steal your energy. However, on occasion you will encounter people who life has not been kind to. Tragedy, loss and poor circumstances can often bring people down despite their outlook on life. Please don't choose to ignore these people just because their unfortunate conditions put a damper on your energy. Remember that while people influence your energy level, you also influence other people's energy. You can help people take a step up in life by choosing to positively impact them. Chogyam Trungpa said, "Compassion automatically invites you to relate with people because you no longer regard people as a drain on your energy."

Try to think about compassion the way a dog does. One reason people find a dog such a great comfort is because when you're feeling down and out, they never try to find out why. They just sit with you and give you the support of their presence. George Eliot once said, "We long for an affection altogether ignorant of our faults. Heaven has accorded this to us in the uncritical canine attachment."

By empathizing with people, you will not only help them regain some of their former energy, you will learn just how rewarding it is to help someone else. In the future, you may need someone to do the same for you. If you're lucky enough you will have both human and canine companions.

"Make the most of yourself, for that is all there is of you."
   - Ralph Waldo Emerson

CHAPTER SEVEN: REinvest in You

You've made the decision to take more control of your life and build even greater momentum towards achieving greater happiness and fulfillment. That's great. Just remember that success and happiness are sustained by continually investing in your own personal growth and joy for life.

James Allen said, "You are today where your thoughts have brought you; you will be tomorrow where your thoughts take you." Joy and happiness are the result of purposeful investment in your own well-being and planning for your someday. Without taking careful consideration of whom you want to be and where you want to be in your life, you may end up down a path that you didn't intend. It only makes sense to start investing in yourself and your future today.

When I use the word "investment," what comes to mind? Most people respond with money. We invest our money to build wealth, prepare for retirement or have a safety net in case of emergencies. We spend a lot of time and energy worrying about how these investments are performing. We are quick to gauge our success by looking at quarterly financial statements. We compare our bank account balances, retirement saving plans, stocks, bonds, assets and the value of our homes. We place great importance on these numbers because we can easily determine whether or not they have been a good investment. The results are measurable and, without a doubt, they are all important investments, but are these the investments that really matter?

Over the years, you have probably heard over and over again that the best thing you can do is invest in a home or a solid career. Both will pay big dividends in the future and add security. If you take a look at your net worth, you could argue that your home is your best financial asset. You could also reason that if you have a steady job and a rewarding career, it will provide income for years and possibly decades to come. But in the end, these assets pale in comparison to your greatest asset, yourself. Investing in you can yield returns far superior than any other investment.

You are an asset. Think about that for a moment. *You are an asset*. You are an asset to the company you work for, you're an asset to your significant other, and let me tell you that it goes without saying, but if you have children, you are an incredible asset to them. You are an asset to the sports team you play on, the church group you belong to, the neighbors you live beside, the community you live in and those you interact with on a daily basis. You are an asset to more people than you know.

Imagine looking in a mirror. What do you see? Do you see a person of value or do you doubt your worth? How do you think your family sees you? How valuable are you to them? You are an asset; there is no doubt about it. You make a difference every day with your words and actions. You build yourself up or you tear yourself down. You build others up or you tear them down. You are in control. So why not invest in those things that bring you the greatest results.

Notice I keep using the word "investing." Spending and investing are not the same things. Spending is simply the act of exchanging value. You go to a store to buy a jacket. You give the clerk a sufficient amount of money and receive a coat of the equivalent value. Investing on the other hand creates value. After the initial cost is paid for, you keep getting value without putting in any further input. If you invest your money, you're expecting to earn more money over time. Through dividends, money you invest in stocks actually earns you more money each year without you having to do any work.

Investing money isn't a new idea. We have all done it at some time. However, few of us think about personal investments. Does your time earn more time? Does your energy earn more energy? Do the investments you make in yourself pay out worthwhile dividends or are you blindly investing in whatever is in front of you hoping that it will grow and not crash? Do you even know? This is the most important question you can ask yourself. Do you know if your investments in yourself are paying off? Are they adding value to you and your life?

Investing in you is important on both a professional and personal level. These two aspects of your life, as we discussed in regards to your balance, are intertwined. Investing in your professional life will impact aspects of your personal life and investing in your personal life will undoubtedly help your professional life. To invest in your personal self, you have to determine what is important to you. A vision, personal mission statement and goals will help you identify this. It is imperative that if you haven't already created a plan, then you should spend time doing it now. Without a personal plan geared towards your success and happiness, then you might as well be opening the paper to the investment pages, closing your eyes and pointing. You're at the mercy of your lack of knowledge and there is no guarantee that your investment will pay off.

You know what matters most to you. Is it spending time with family and friends? Staying active and experiencing new adventures? Helping others through community work? Spending time doing your hobbies? With these thoughts in mind, how often do you get to spend time doing these things? If you're like most people, the answer is probably not enough. How often have you said that life is too short? You should be taking this to heart and making the most out of each and every day. Think of what well-known motivational speaker Zig Ziglar said, "The definition of success is getting many of the things money can buy and all the things money can't buy." Invest accordingly.

This past holiday, Jane and I were reminiscing about how fast the time has gone by. Our oldest, Evan, was 20 years old, but it seemed like yesterday I was reading him *Where the Wild Things Are*. Life is too brief to be caught in a rut or stuck running around constantly trying to meet deadlines or make more money.

You need to make time for the things you love now. That's why last Christmas my gifts were focused around personal investment. For example, I gave Jane snowshoes. Of course, there were two pairs, one for her and one for me. That way, I was investing in our quality time and our relationship, as well as getting exercise at the same time. That's a good personal investment in my books.

I surprised my father and son with tickets to the NFL ProBowl. They both love football and I got to spend a few days with just them. It was three generations together creating a special experience that will be remembered and enjoyed for years to come. I call that a great investment because it was important to me at that point in my life.

Both gifts strengthened my relationships with those I love, creating memories and a bond that will last years.

Trust me when I tell you though, there's no shortage of tasks and deadlines at work right now. I'm extremely busy. It's so easy for me to make an excuse as to why I don't have time to invest in myself. There's always a reason to put off those personal things I want to do for the sake of getting another work project out the door or meeting another client deadline. You've been there. You know you have and I know you have. However, scheduling personal investment time is just as important as meeting a deadline. Personally, I find that investing in me brings out more creativity and energy at work. I feel less stressed, so it results in greater productivity. This is the connection between personal and professional investment. When you devote time to one you get a return in the other.

Whatever it is you wish you could be doing, find a way to make it happen now. This is easier said than done, but it can be accomplished if you put your mind to it. I know changing everything all at once is not reality. We all have responsibilities. That's a fact. However, far too often I hear people use the excuse that they have to sacrifice their own personal wants to meet those of others. Are you like that? Are you sacrificing what you really want to do for the sake of helping other people with their needs? It's time for that to change. Don't view personal investment as a want. Personal investment is a need. In order to be the best you can be you need to invest in yourself. Start with gradual changes. Today I want you to make a commitment to find one thing to incorporate into your regular schedule that you love to do.

The cold, hard truth is that you have to make time. Stop making excuses and make a decision today to do something that invests in you and your happiness. If you can make time to run to the grocery store every week, don't tell me you can't set aside half an hour to do something that you actually enjoy. You need to invest in you. It's all about balance. Your life is filled with responsibilities, deadlines, projects and tasks, but you can't let these things control you. You need to invest in creating some personal time.

You may have noticed that I continuously refer to habits. We are habitual creatures. So much so that we convince ourselves that we don't have time for ourselves. Our habits can influence our thoughts and our actions. The solution is simple: invest in yourself and your happiness by creating new habits. Do it gradually, even if it's just 30 minutes a day or week. The more you can introduce things you love into your life, the happier you'll be. Your happiness will begin to impact the other areas of your life. You'll perform better at work, you'll feel better about yourself, you'll have more confidence to try new things and you'll have better relationships with your family and friends. Overall, you'll become a greater asset to everyone you interact with. All the time you put in at work and all the effort to save money for the future don't mean a whole lot if you aren't investing in what makes you happy so you can enjoy it.

If you were walking in a shopping mall and saw a penny on the ground, would you stop to pick it up? You might say for good luck, but it is unlikely you'd pick it up for its value as currency. It is just a penny after all. What does a penny buy these days? I bet many of you would say you wouldn't even bother picking up a nickel or even a dime. The value has to be higher before you would go through the effort of bending down.

Why not a penny? We don't see much worth in a penny. But I can still hear my parents saying, "If you take care of your pennies, you never have to worry about the dollars. If you always spend a penny less than you make, you'll never have a money problem." Every denomination is made up of pennies. There are five pennies in a nickel, ten in a dime, twenty-five in a quarter, a hundred in a dollar. Be penny-wise.

Don't just put all your time and effort into the big ticket items you can only enjoy once in a while. Invest in the little daily things that you may not think are worth much, but when you add them all up they increase both the quality and quantity of joy in your life. They create good investing habits. Take care of the little things and you will never have to worry about the big ones – they will happen naturally.

You've probably heard many times before that you don't have anything if you don't have your health. You can make all the improvements to other areas of your life, but in order to enjoy them, you need to take care of your body and mind first. Sure, money is important, but without your health, it's worthless. I know all you're hearing right now is nagging because you think I'm going to talk about dieting and exercise and cutting out all the fun stuff in life. And I agree, none of that sounds like fun, but when I talk about improving your health, I'm not talking about making drastic changes overnight. Your health is impacted by habits you've developed over the course of years and they can be hard to break, so it's best to make small changes over time that will lead to healthier habits. Denis Waitley said, "Habits are like comfortable beds. They are easy to get into, but difficult to get out of." You need to start rolling towards the edge of the bed and I have five simple areas where you can easily invest in your health and they will eventually make dramatic impacts on the quality of your happiness.

Get More Sleep

Yes, I'm repeating myself (and I'll do it again), but this is important. We live in a busy world that never seems to rest and getting caught up in this busyness can take a toll on sleep. With the increase in social networking demands due to the likes of Facebook and Twitter and the expectations surrounding instant response time through the internet, Blackberry's and iphones combined with TV and extracurricular activities, the day doesn't end when you come home from work. This added stress and lack of downtime can really cut into your sleep and cause havoc in your life.

One of my colleagues says her friend's teenage sister even sleeps with her cell phone on her pillow so she won't miss any calls or texts. Granted, she's a teenager, but this is the next generation, already tied to technology. She will even wake up and text people back at 2 a.m. There are no longer any boundaries.

Do you find yourself hitting the snooze button each morning or struggling to find the strength to even swing your feet over the edge and onto the floor? Do you find you can't concentrate until you've had your first or second cup of coffee in the morning? Do you just wish you could curl up for a nap in the afternoon while you are at work?

Wherever I go, people complain about how tired they are. I know, I hear you. There are only 24 hours in a day and you already can't find enough time to get everything done. So how can you be expected to get even more sleep? The cold, hard fact is you have to in order to improve your life. Think about all the time you waste when you aren't completely focused or are working inefficiently because you're fighting the urge to fall asleep. You need to redirect this time that is wasted because you're tired and put it into getting more zzz's.

The following are a few tips to help you change your habits and bounce out of that comfortable bed in the morning– literally.

Your bedroom is designed for only two things, sleep being one and we all know the other and it isn't watching TV. Remove any televisions from your room so you don't stay up later than you normally would because you just want to see how the show ends. Start going to bed 30 minutes earlier or go to bed earlier and read a book until you are tired. Never discuss finances, problems at work or home while lying in bed. These discussions cause anxiety to rise and the brain to race, making it harder to quiet your mind and body for a restful sleep.

It's also important to limit the amount of caffeine you drink in the evening. Studies show that it takes eight hours to reduce the amount of caffeine in your body by half. That means while your body is already working hard at restoring your systems from the day, it now has an additional workload while you are trying to sleep. Your body needs rest to repair and rejuvenate you from the stresses of the day and prepare you to face the challenges of tomorrow, don't give it more than it can handle just because you like a coffee after dinner. Drink decaf instead.

By creating better sleep habits, you will wake up feeling better. Your body will be rested and you can make better use of your waking hours, not to mention the improvement to your overall health.

Exercise More

Yes, you need to get more exercise. Again, this does not mean you need to sign up at the local gym and dedicate two hours per day to the gods of sweat. However, if that works for you, please be my guest. Exercise can be as simple as a walk after dinner, a yoga class or a fun family activity like my snowshoes.

But beware of letting your mind make all of the decisions when choosing an activity. Don't ignore the abilities and limitations of your body. I learned this lesson the hard way when my son and I were at the gym a few years back.

We prefer to lift weights as neither of us enjoys cardiovascular workouts, but we understand their importance on our overall health. So one day, instead of riding the stationary bikes or jogging on the treadmill, we decided to hit the basketball court and run off a little testosterone. Although Evan is taller than I am, over 25 years younger and quite the athlete, I played a lot of basketball in my younger days and I dare say, was pretty good. Hence the problem.

There I was, standing at the top of the key, bouncing the ball at my side. The only thing between me and the net was my son, daring me to give it my best shot. His taunts got the better of me and I was determined to show him that his dad wasn't some old geezer. I drove toward the net, my shoulder down. I effortlessly leaped into the air, double pumping my shot under than over his outstretched arms and let the ball masterfully roll off the tips of my fingers, banking it off the backboard and into the net.

Or at least that's how I saw it in my head. To be truthful, I'm not entirely sure what actually happened, but I do know my ego took a massive blow when, after I took my shot (which fell dismally short of the hoop), I was lying on the court with my son standing over me, laughing so hard that tears were rolling down his face. After catching his breath, he described, between bursts of glee, how I had looked with my red face and bulging eyes, contorting my body and flailing my arms. I thought I was reliving my glory days but I only succeeded in looking like a mess and my body felt the effects for days afterwards. And Evan couldn't stop telling everyone about his dad, the "superstar" basketball player. Too bad he was under 18 at the time and I was legally obliged to keep him out of harm's way.

The lesson is that, while exercise will increase your overall well-being and improve your ability to enjoy the other investments in your life, you need to make sure you obey the limits of your body. Align your thoughts and actions, there is no use injuring yourself trying to be healthier.

My son and I still like to horse around, whether it is on the basketball court, tossing the football or throwing one another into the river off the dock. And yes, for an older guy, I still win once in a while.

Eat Better

Don't worry; I'm not talking about going on a drastic diet and cutting ten pounds in one month. There is no need to embark on an all grapefruit regime, but a few changes to your diet can go a long way, such as eating a healthy breakfast. Please don't skip breakfast. It provides you with the energy you need for the day. Time and again, we get dressed and showered, grab a piece of toast and run out the door. More often than not, the toast gets half eaten and then tossed when we snag our first cup of coffee. The key to making a habit out of eating breakfast is to take the time to sit down and eat it. This way you won't get preoccupied by other things and realize you left your toast on the roof of the car when you were looking for your keys.

Be more conscious about what you're eating and make an effort to incorporate small changes here and there. Eat according to the habits of earlier generations – big breakfasts, medium lunches and smaller dinners. If you drink a few sodas each day, start replacing one with another beverage. My daughter, Hannah, was shocked when she found out how much sugar was in one can. Ideally, you should replace it with water since our bodies easily become dehydrated throughout the day. Over time, you will find that you crave soda less and in the process you will cut a lot of calories out of your diet.

I strongly recommend consulting a nurtritionalist, if you are able, so you can learn how to eat properly for your body type. This can make a huge difference in your energy levels. If you can't, just eat sensibly and don't overindulge, it's that simple.

Go to Your Doctor

You're probably wondering why you need to go see a doctor more when you are taking better care of yourself. A healthy person should need to visit the doctor less, right? While this is true, regular checkups are a must to ensure you stay healthy. Nothing beats a preventative approach to your health. Unfortunately, too many people wait until something is wrong before seeing a doctor and this can easily derail them from life. Be proactive.

Remember that an ounce of prevention is worth a pound of cure.

To make things easier, check to see if you can schedule yearly appointments after each checkup and if not, put reminders on your calendar at home or work.

Build in Quiet or Creative Time

You have to take care of your mind just as much as your body. Meditations, reading a book, going for a walk, writing in a journal or taking up a hobby are all ways to invest in your mental health. Your mind needs to recharge and revitalize from the noise and stress of the day. This will impact your overall well-being.

Many people are heading towards health problems later in life because they refuse to build in the right healthy habits today. These problems can cause financial hardships and relationship issues that reduce the quality of your life as you get older. From an investment standpoint, it is much more cost-effective to focus on staying healthy than to take action once something's gone wrong. If you invest in your good health today, you'll perform better at work, you'll have more energy to spend with your family and friends and on your goals. In general, you'll feel better about yourself and happier while building the opportunity to fully enjoy your investments in the future. It's win-win.

Investing in you isn't all about work and sacrifice. It is equally important to invest in what I call the Indulgences of Life. These indulgences are what you would like to do, but tend to sacrifice or rationalize because of other pressing priorities. I want you to change your way of thinking when it comes to these. Often, people see them as something to do only every once in a while. They do not see them as adding value to their lives; they are treats or luxuries. Don't do this. These activities have long-term benefits associated with them – they reduce stress, increase your sense of well-being, allow you to put things into perspective easier and give you a new lease on life.

They could include treating yourself to a massage, a day at the spa, a night on the town or taking a vacation once a year instead of sitting in the backyard or doing work around the house during your time off. It doesn't need to be an expensive trip. It could be as simple as a weekend away hiking in the mountains or reconnecting with someone special. Indulgences are important. You know the saying about all work and no play. It makes you and your life pretty dull. Have a little fun and go out and play. These are your rewards.

For years I always wanted to swim with the dolphins. It was a dream that started when I was a child and I carried it with me into adulthood like a penny in my pocket. Every once in a while, I'd take that penny out, think how great it would be and say someday I'm going to do that, then I'd put it back in my pocket. I was perpetually too busy to book the adventure, until one day I looked at that penny and said I was going to invest it in myself because I deserved it. I work hard every other day of the year and I needed that trip for myself and my wife. And you know what? It was unbelievably rewarding. My swim was so satisfying and invigorating that my energy levels were at an all-time high for months afterwards.

Now, when I'm stressed at work, I can look at the picture I keep of it in my office and it automatically takes me back and makes me feel better. Since then I make sure I plan to invest in indulgences as rewards for my hard work and to share time with the people I love. What pennies are you carrying around in your pockets that you could start investing?

Investments in yourself not only create memories for years to come, but encourage those closest to you to want to share in and reinforce those great feelings. Jane and I could not stop talking about this life changing swim, so much so that on our last family vacation, Hannah and Evan insisted we share the experience with them. Hannah wanted the full dolphin encounter for her 18th birthday. She was able to hold onto the dolphin's dorsal fin while it swam and also had the dolphin push her across the water. When she was finished, the whole family swam and fed manatees, the gentle cows of the sea. This is another memory I will cherish forever. My pennies had multiplied.

Life is serious. You have many responsibilities and pressures. Play has a way of putting life back into balance. Whether it is going on a picnic, playing paintball, learning how to ballroom dance or taking cooking lessons, you need to involve play in your life. Seemingly simple investments like a day at the beach or amusement park pay huge dividends by keeping joy alive in your life. I think you need to play at least once a month. Once a week is better, but if you plan for at least once a month you will feel the benefits. Schedule it into your calendar at home or your day planner at work just like it's any other appointment and make plans accordingly.

As you invest in indulgences and play, it is important to continually invest in your skills so you don't become obsolete. I'm not just referring to work-related skills either, but life skills as well. All of us have a certain skill set, often based on what we do at work, our education, hobbies and day-to-day experiences. Employers, of course, tend to be interested primarily in work-related skills – what you can do or offer them. You'll see this in the job description. Some of these will be very specific to particular jobs, but it is often the other skills, the so-called transferable skills, that can propel you to greater success. These are more of the attitudinal, motivational and relationship building skills that you use in your career *and* life. Your priority for self-investment should be to continually improve these ones. They include such things as communication, negotiation, listening and speaking skills. Time spent staying sharp in these areas will always pay off.

Completing a skills inventory is an easy exercise you should do a few times a year. This will show you what you currently are capable of and what you need to work on. To do this, dedicate 10 to 15 minutes of uninterrupted time where you can sit down with a sheet of paper. Divide the paper into two halves, one for your personal skills and one for your professional skills. This way you create the entire package. It is also very rewarding to see all of your skills on paper.

Once this is done, write out what you want to accomplish over the next year and then review your skills to see if there are any gaps. If there are, ask yourself if you can develop these skills with a little time or money. For example, if you are dreaming of starting a new career or side business, what skills would you need to do this? Be sure to update your list at least twice a year.

Investing in new skills doesn't have to be expensive. Nowadays, there are plenty of ways to get the information that you require. You can read a book, take a course at a local community college or find a program online. You just need to identify what skill you want to acquire and then get creative and actively look for a solution. As someone once shared with me – Don't be afraid to invest in yourself. It's not selfish, it's self-full.

When a puppy is born, we don't pass judgment on it because it can't see. We know it is still growing. When we bring the puppy home, we do not criticize it when it pees on the floor or chews the furniture; we understand that it needs our guidance and attention. When it first escapes out of the front door and runs down the street, we may curse, but we know as we drag it back home, that it is still learning. When the dog grows old, and is no longer able to climb the stairs, we don't disparage it. We help make it comfortable. We give the dog the care it needs at each stage of its life. And in return, it provides us with loyalty and unfailing love. This is the way you should treat yourself. One of my university professors always used to say, "I never 'am,' I'm always 'becoming.' "

Life is a journey. You are where you are as a result of the decisions you have made in your life. Take stock of all the great things you have accomplished. Live in the moment and enjoy all that life is bringing to you right now. As you continue on your journey through life, ask yourself what you are doing to nourish your growth. Are you feeding you? Treat yourself as you treat your dog. Know that sometimes you will make mistakes, but if you invest the time and energy into making yourself better you will live a more rewarding life. Invest in those things that move you closer to your own goals and happiness. It's in you for the taking.

*"How did it get so late so soon?
It's night before its afternoon.
December is here before its June.
My goodness how the time has flewn.
How did it get so late so soon?"*
- Dr. Suess

CHAPTER EIGHT: REalize the Moment

I'm Italian (and Polish on my dad's side) and my mom is your quintessential Italian mama. She loves to cook and fuss over everyone. When I'm around she's always asking me if I need anything, if everything is okay at home, if the kids are good, and, of course, wondering if I'm getting enough to eat.

Both my parents are wonderful people, unassuming and always willing to lend a hand. When they befriended a couple with a young son from their church who had just moved to their city, I was not surprised that they became surrogate grandparents to the little boy. They didn't even hesitate when the parents asked them to do them a huge favor and look after him when they were in the hospital for the birth of their new baby. My parents took this request to heart, rarely leaving the house, and when they did, ensuring they called the young couple with the number of the place where they would be. They even chose to miss their granddaughter's graduation, as distraught as it made my mother, for fear that they wouldn't be home for the call.

The other day I was visiting them and wanted to take them out for dinner.

"No, no," my mother said, fluttering her hand at me. "You don't need to do that; I'll just cook you something."

But I insisted and we finally settled on the Fish Market that they wanted to try. Of course, as soon as the menu arrived at our table, I could tell that my mother was scanning for the cheapest dish on it.

"Mom," I said. "Order whatever you want. Let *me* treat *you* for once."

When the food arrived, my parents started to tell me about a trip they were planning for the fall that would take them through Poland, Prague and Budapest. As I watched them talk about it, I noticed small glances they were giving one another, looks filled with love, friendship and a little sadness. It dawned on me that they both believed this might be the last big trip they would take together.

My dad has cancer and my mom's health isn't what it used to be. The last time I visited, she was distressed because my dad had told her that if he goes first she needs to sell their house because she shouldn't be living there all alone with the stairs. They always put each other's needs and concerns above their own.

With their mortality facing them, I've noticed the care and consideration they take with the small things in their lives. My mom is always hugging and kissing me now (even more than usual!). The last time they sent gifts for Evan's birthday and Hannah's graduation, they included pictures of the kids when they were little that they'd kept. It was like, with these small sentimental offerings, they were trying to remind their grandkids not to grow up too fast and wish their lives away, but to enjoy the time they had, right here and now because it goes so quickly.

It reminded me of the lyrics to a song by Kenny Chesney about an old man turning 102 talking about how quickly the years rush past. It's called "Don't Blink." It goes:

> just like that you're six years old and you take a nap and you
> Wake up and you're twenty-five and your high school sweetheart becomes your wife
> Don't blink
> Just might miss your babies growin' like mine did
> Turning into moms and dads; next thing you know your better half of fifty years is there in bed
> And you're praying God takes you instead
> Trust me friend, one hundred years goes faster than you think
> So don't Blink

The lyrics continue with the old man saying, "Best start putting first things first, cause when your hour glass runs out of sand you can't flip it over and start again. Take every breath God gives you for what it's worth."

A few weeks ago, Hannah came into my office in tears after paying her respects at the wake of a beloved teacher from her school who had lost his valiant battle with cancer at the age of just 34. He was active, involved in playing and coaching sports, a teacher with a positive attitude, always willing to help a student out. He was just recently married and looking forward to a lifetime of memories still ahead of him. But life can be so cold.

When Hannah first heard that her teacher's cancer was spreading through his body, she took a school shirt and turned it into a pillow. She sent it to the teacher's home with a note that said she and the whole school were thinking and praying for him.

At the wake, when the father saw it was Hannah who had made the pillow, he told her she was a Godsend. Apparently, his son had kept it with him all the time. Even in grief, my daughter understood the impact of one selfless act. I told her to realize and appreciate this moment. We may not always understand why bad things happen, but we must learn the lesson in order to realize how valuable the time we share together is and to make the most of it.

About a week after that wake, I came home from work and found a box of pictures sitting on the kitchen table. Jane had decided to clear away some of the clutter around the house when she came across the photos. I stashed my bag in my office, sat down at the table and decided to flip through some of them before dinner. It didn't take long before I was calling my family over and we all started going through the pictures, reminiscing about times past. "Remember when we went there?" Hannah said. "I can't believe we did that!" Evan exclaimed. "What a great time," Jane sighed. These statements came pouring out of our mouths as all the emotions from these fond experiences resurfaced.

When my children were born, they had four grandparents and seven great-grandparents. If that wasn't enough, my son was the first grandson and my daughter is still the only granddaughter. I wonder how they didn't end up spoiled rotten! We were extremely fortunate to say that on many occasions we had four generations in one room. The pictures in the box were reminders of all the special moments we shared with our loved ones. Disney World with my parents, outings with Jane's parents, teasing and laughter with uncles, the obligatory family pictures from weddings and graduations that everyone complains about at the time, but cherish later, and the wide-eyed wonderment as great-grandparents held them as babies for the first time, their wrinkled hands, grown unaccustomed to baby-holding, cradling the new life oh-so carefully. And of course, the standard naked baby pictures that I will forever keep in order to haunt them on their wedding days and laugh at with my own grandchildren someday.

Life has a way of getting busy and if you're not careful, it is easy to lose sight of all the little moments that happen every day that take on more significance later in life; the ones that bring tears to your eyes and smiles to your lips like the pictures in that old cardboard box did for my family as we crowded around the kitchen table on what otherwise would have been just another Tuesday evening.

I think we let the most important things slip through our fingers. We don't cherish them enough as we should. We take for granted the simple things that can bring so much joy to our lives, expecting that they will always be there when we need them.

My parents got a dog named Ah So Lovely Ting Ting when I was young. I know, an outrageous name. Just imagine going out on the step and calling that dog home! We nicknamed her Tingy instead. Tingy was with us until the ripe old age of 16. By the time she passed away, I had already moved out onto my own and gotten married. I'll never forget the day she died.

My parents were supposed to be stopping by our house in Barrie, where we lived at the time, on their way back to Burlington from the cottage. It was Mother's Day and we were looking forward to having dinner together. As always, Tingy was traveling with them.

I was expecting them for a certain time, so when that time came and went I started to get worried. Finally, hours after they should have arrived, the phone rang. I was concerned that they hadn't called earlier to say they were going to be delayed and was upset when I heard my mom on the other end. That feeling vanished instantly when I heard the tears in her voice. I asked what had happened and she told me that on their way to our house, Tingy had a heart attack as she lay on my mom's lap. They rushed her to the vet's, but she passed away.

My mom was devastated. That dog had been their friend for years. Always counted upon to meet them at the door, ride with them in the car and sit with them on the couch in the evening. Only now that she was no longer there did my mom see how large a hole one little dog could leave in her life.

We take many more things for granted than just our pets. A lot of us take the most significant things in our lives for granted because they are always there. Only when they are absent do we realize what a difference they made for us. How much happiness they brought us.

Pictures are great. They allow you to relive moments that brought you joy and delight, but the real thing is much more satisfying. Sister Corita Kent said, "Love the moment and the energy of the moment will spread beyond all boundaries." Start prioritizing the things in your life and "putting first things first" give them the attention they deserve. You are graced with the same 24 hours in a day, the same 1440 minutes, the same 86 400 seconds as everyone else. You have no more or less. The big difference is how you choose to use this time.

My son uses a familiar phrase around the house when asked to do something, "I'll do it tomorrow." Occasionally, he adds "I promise" to the end of it as if those two words will reinforce his message. I've told him time and again my frustration in regard to his "I'll do it tomorrow, I promise" promise because many times it remains unfulfilled. It's not intentional (not always), something will distract him or he'll forget or he'll find something else to do. I think I get frustrated because I fear that this will turn into a habit for him. I hear people saying "I'll do it tomorrow," but then tomorrow never seems to come for them.

Realizing the moment involves not only appreciating what is happening in the present, but also appreciating the value of time and being able to act in the moment as well. Too many experiences are missed just because we are not in the present. We are too busy living in the future, thinking about appointments, tasks and events next week or month.

There is a quote by Alice Morse Earle that goes: "The clock is running. Make the most of today. Time waits for no man. Yesterday is history. Tomorrow is a mystery. Today is a gift. That's why it is called the present." I think too many of us are forgetting to appreciate the gift of time. Right now, list five unique, special or memorable things that happened to you last week. Too hard? What about some of the best experiences in your life? If you struggle with these questions, you're not opening your gift and realizing the moment.

Quiet time helps ground people in the moment. Personally, I love waking up early in the morning on the weekend. I quietly slip out of bed in order to not wake Jane and I'll take Lilly and Molly and the three of us will go out and sit on the deck overlooking the glistening calmness of the river. I sit in my Adirondack chair and just watch the morning mist dancing in the rays of the rising sun. I believe my dogs understand the importance of this morning quiet time. They will curl up on the deck by my feet or sit in my lap. Any other time of the day, if they saw a squirrel, person or even a leaf blowing in the breeze, they might bark or chase after it, but not on a weekend morning. It's time to soak in life. It's in these quiet moments I reflect upon the past week, thank God for the gifts in my life and just enjoy the day.

Many people tell me they struggle with silence. Some people just aren't comfortable with being alone with their thoughts. When they jump in the car they turn on the radio. When they come home to an empty house, they flick on the TV. The thought of silence is discomforting.

As discomforting as it might seem initially, you and I, we need silence. It can come in different ways for different people, it may be going for a walk, spending time in the garden, writing in a journal or just quiet time on a deck. However it comes into your life you need to incorporate it so you can learn how to realize your own moments. You need silence to ground you in the moment.

How often has something happened in your life that smacks you and yells, "Listen up, knucklehead!" You need these AH HAs. Life has so much to offer you. You can't ignore life or waste the moments it offers being in a rush to get to the next task.

Don't believe me? How often throughout your life have you:

- Wondered where the months or years have gone?

- Felt like there was something bigger out there for you?

- Walked on a warm beach and wondered what took you so long to get there?

- Wanted to just sell it all and open a café in the Caribbean?

- Felt relieved that Lady Luck watched over you?

- Had your breath taken away by something?

- Just sat and watched a child sleep peacefully in the middle of the night?

That, my friend, is life gently tapping you on the shoulder and telling you to slow down and be grateful for your life.

This can be disguised in many ways. Scuba diving was one such vehicle for me. I got my diving license when I was still in university. It was something I'd always wanted to do and when the opportunity presented itself I took it. I did my final open water dive to get my official license in the cold waters of Georgian Bay in Tobermory, Ontario. After that, I dove at our family cottage in Kawagama Lake. The feeling of weightlessness and the awe of experiencing life beneath the surface is definitely surreal.

It was my first ocean dive where life tapped me on the shoulder in a big way. We were about a mile off the island of Cozumel, Mexico when the dive instructor told us to jump in. Although it was 26 years ago, I can still remember vividly the feeling of my heart pounding like it was yesterday.

The ocean was much warmer than the Ontario waters I was used to. There were vibrant colors from the fish and coral. I remember my diving partner pointing to his depth gauge that read 50 feet and then pointing up. I was completely amazed to easily see the clouds in the sky above us. The water was so clear that visibility went on forever. I was in sensory overload. Never in my wildest dreams had I pictured something so beautiful and wonderful in my life that far.

And it got better. We fed giant groupers (large fish that can grow to lengths of over a meter and weight up to 100 kg) hot dog wieners right from our hands! I got close enough to a sea turtle for me to hitch a short ride. It was exhilarating.

Then came my moment, when life told me to slow down. We were floating with the current below us and I folded my hands in front of me and stopped kicking my fins. I took long slow breaths and let the current do all the work. I drifted effortlessly along, soaking it up. I was just there. It is an experience, a feeling in my life that I use as a reference point when I need to remember how to live in the moment when life has gotten hectic and out of control.

I've had many moments like this throughout my life:

- When I proposed to my wife using a Care Bear.

- When I held my son for the first time after he was born, overwhelmed with joy and the awesome responsibility I had been handed.

- The first day I walked into my own office as a business owner.

- Getting the news from the doctor that my wife would be okay after her horrific car accident.

- The first time I swam with a dolphin.

- Every time I lost a grandparent.

- My parents' 50th wedding anniversary.

- Sitting in the stands watching my son play quarterback for his high school football team.

- Waving goodbye as my daughter, my baby, left for France for two weeks.

- When my father told me he had cancer.

Life deals you experiences that force you to stop and take stock of what is happening in your life. It awakens the realization of what is truly important. It always leaves you a choice. Do you learn from the lesson or do you go back to your old habits and wait for the next tap, missing out on the many special moments in between?

The older I get, the more open I am to these life experiences. With age comes wisdom and awareness (most of the time). Life doesn't have to tap very hard now that I've learned to keep an eye out for things to be grateful for. It's much easier to realize and appreciate the moments this way and it brings much more joy into my life.

Realizing the moment is not just about the events that come your way that bring joy and excitement into your life; it is also the people you share them with. An appreciation of the moment is also an appreciation of the people in the moment. Far too often, we let the busyness of life act as an excuse to drift away from people. Or we let past grudges, bad feelings and disappointments sour a relationship. Harriet Beecher Stowe said, "The bitterest tears shed over graves are for words left unsaid and for deeds left undone."

In order to live life fully, you need to appreciate those who live it with you. Life would be very lonely indeed without company. Don't wait for special occasions to tell people what they mean to you. Life is a special occasion and you'll never get another life. Zachary Scott said, "As you grow older, you'll find the only things you regret are the things you didn't do." Don't let any of these regrets be not telling someone how much they meant to you or allowing a petty argument or grudge to keep you away from the people who can add meaning and happiness to your life.

Some of us are fortunate enough to know when we are going to die and are able to evaluate our lives and take the time to tell those we love what they mean to us and mend fences that have been left in disrepair. However, for most of us, we will never have this opportunity, thus it is important to take stock of the people in your life each day. An anonymous person once said that you should present your family and friends with their eulogies now because they won't be able to hear how much you love them and appreciate them when they or you are gone.

It's never too late to start realizing the moments and to appreciate and be grateful for what you have in the present. My wish for my children is that they will adopt this approach now when they are young. Their view of the world and acceptance of others will be a lot brighter.

In January, Evan and I flew to Florida to visit my parents for a week. We used the tickets for the ProBowl being held in Miami for the first time, which was only a two hour drive from my parent's winter house that I'd given my dad and son that Christmas. Three generations together to take in the experience. It was a weekend to remember.

But what impressed me the most was the days after the ProBowl. The weather in Florida was colder and wetter than normal for January and with a nice pool outside and beaches a short drive away, you'd think our spirits would be dampened by not being able to take advantage of them. Instead, we played Euchre for hours on end, my father and son challenging my mother and I hand after hand. Evan and my mom kept us laughing, Evan with his one liners and my mother as she continually tried to curse them with the evil eye so they would get unlucky cards and lose.

When my son and I were flying home, with the lunches my mother had packed for us stashed in our carry-ons, I told him I was sorry the weather had been so bad and we couldn't do anything he'd wanted. With a big smile on his face he said, "Are you kidding? I couldn't have asked for a better week. Hanging out with Grandma and Grandpa was awesome!"

Even though he still constantly says "I'll do it tomorrow, I promise" I know he realizes how important these moments in life are and the people we share them with. Life is good in his mind and I hope it will always stay that way.

Your life is your playground. It is your choice to play in it or to sit on the edge, kicking pebbles and wishing you could join in. Take time to stop and enjoy the results of your life, find joy in the small things and be grateful for where you are or you will never fully realize the richness life has to offer. If this isn't enough to cause you to take more stock of your life, heed the words of Hector

Berlioz: "Time is a great teacher, but unfortunately it kills all its pupils."

I find that songs often have best advice hidden in their lyrics. At the beginning of this chapter, I wrote about a country song, now I'm going to end it with a rock song that I think you should take to heart. The song is called "If Today was Your Last Day," by Nickelback:

> My best friend gave me the best advice
> He said each day's a gift and not a given right
> Leave no stone unturned, leave your fears behind
> And try to take the path less traveled by
> That first step you take is the longest stride.

CONCLUSION

Back in 1990, Jane and I invited some friends to stay at our family cottage. Evan was about 16 months old and we wanted to spend some quality time away with our friends. Jane started to feel ill early that evening and as the night progressed, so did her pain and discomfort. We knew something must be wrong and made the decision to head to the hospital. We left our son with our friends, jumped in the boat and proceeded the six miles down the lake to the marina. Once we got to the marina, it was another 45 minute drive to the hospital in Huntsville.

On the way to the marina, Jane's pain severely increased to the point where she started to pass out. At one stage, she actually thought she was going to die and said good-bye to me. You can only imagine how I was feeling. As I raced into the dock slip at the marina, Jane was semi-conscious. I ran to the marina house for help, pounded on the door and yelled for someone to call for an ambulance. At this point I was afraid to even move her out of the boat.

After what seemed like an eternity, the paramedics arrived and as they were checking Jane, she suddenly and unexpectedly opened her eyes and said she felt better. The paramedics kept monitoring her vitals until they returned to normal. Puzzled by the drastic change, they recommended we still go to the hospital, but Jane was worried about Evan and said she felt 100% better, so we decided to head back to the cottage and drive to the hospital the next day for a checkup.

On the way back, thunder clouds began moving in ahead of us and we could see lightning streaking across the darkened sky. *Not to worry*, I thought to myself, *I know this lake like the back of my hand.* After all, I'd been boating on it for years.

As we rounded the final point that would set us in direct line with the island, we were hit by the storm. The wind whipped itself into a frenzy and we were soaked by a torrential downpour. The back of the boat was open and I yelled to Jane to grab the wheel while I put the cover on it. Between me letting go of the wheel and Jane taking control, the waves and wind knocked us off course.

After I secured the cover and took over the wheel, I couldn't understand why we hadn't come to the island yet. The storm was still raging and I couldn't see anything, a scary situation. I knew I was pointing towards the island when the storm hit, so I drove slowly and made sure we both had our life jackets on properly and braced ourselves to hit land… but land never came.

For hours we were tossed around on the lake. We were cold, scared and in the back of my head I kept praying that Jane's earlier symptoms would not return. Finally, the rain let up enough for us to catch a glimpse of land, find a dock and tie up. In the morning light, as we started up the shore looking for shelter from the rain I could see that we were miles from where we were supposed to be.

With this knowledge and the rain finally tampering off, we got back in the boat, cold, hungry and wet and made our way back to our friends and baby. Then it hit me. The answer was right in front of me all along. The compass mounted on the dash. All I had to do was look at the compass and I would have discovered I was off course. The one vital piece of equipment you could always trust when faced with visibility issues on land or in the water. However, in the direness of the situation and with the knowledge that I had been pointed at the island, I never thought to give the compass a glance.

How often are we faced with these situations in life? We have determined where we want to go, but forget to look at our compass and get pulled off course. Finding your true self is just like this. It is all too easy to be blinded by life and drift away from your goals and vision. Storms can easily overcome you. Wind knocks you off balance. Rain wears away at your resilience. Cold weakens your confidence. Waves cause you to lose control. Before you know it, all your energy is gone. To make it to your someday you need to have a trustworthy compass. You need to invest in the skills necessary to get you there. You need to be able to see what you want and believe in it. And along the way, you need to enjoy the small moments that mean so much.

Whenever I think of being lost and not knowing who or where I am, I think of *Alice in Wonderland*. I remember reading it to Hannah when she was little. Arguably one of the best-loved children's books of all time, *Alice in Wonderland* is also a popular story amongst adults. Perhaps this is because we can sympathize with Alice's quest for identity. Her conversation with the Caterpillar resonates with many of us because we can understand Alice's confusion:

> "Who are YOU?" said the Caterpillar. This was not an encouraging opening for a conversation. Alice replied, rather shyly, "I--I hardly know, sir, just at present-- at least I know who I WAS when I got up this morning, but I think I must have been changed several times since then."

We all struggle with the importance and instability of personal identity. Throughout our lives, our identity can change numerous times. We look to others in order to identify ourselves – loving parent, supportive spouse, fun friend, hardworking employee – but far too often we forget to look inside ourselves. We forget to consider what it is that *we* want from ourselves and from our lives.

I always chuckled at the part in *Alice in Wonderland* when members of the jury have to write down their names or they will forget them. However, I think there are times in our lives when we do forget who we are. We forget the dreams we had for ourselves. We forget the potential that our lives hold. I think this is why humans keep dogs as companions. George Bird Evans, in his book *Troubles with Bird Dogs*, wrote:

> I think we are drawn to dogs because they are the uninhibited creatures we might be if we weren't certain we knew better. They fight for honor at the first challenge, make love with no moral restraint, and they do not for all their marvelous instincts appear to know about death. Being such wonderfully uncomplicated beings, they need us to do their worrying.

Dogs are outgoing, open and unreserved. They are spontaneous and live life with abandon. I said at the beginning of this book, that I wrote it to save dogs. That's true. Dogs' lives are so short that they deserve masters who love them and are kind to them and love and kindness come from people who are happy and fulfilled. But I think when we go out and buy a dog that the dog is really saving our lives. They are showing us a new, better way to live life. Gene Hill once commented that whoever said you couldn't buy happiness forgot about puppies and I think he had it right. Could any of us ever expect to have the epitaph George Gordon, Lord Byron wrote for his dog:

> Near this spot are deposited the remains of one who possessed Beauty without Vanity, Strength without Insolence, Courage without Ferocity, and all the Virtues of Man, without his Vices. This Praise, which would be unmeaning Flattery if inscribed over human ashes, is but a just tribute to the Memory of Boatswain, a Dog.

Whenever you are in doubt about the way you are living your life, remember the power that lies inside you. You will always possess the power of RE as your compass. You just need to make the decision to find it and use it. And if you are ever in doubt, look to your four-legged furry friends as guides. And please, reward them for all their work. Give the dog a bone.

ABOUT THE AUTHOR

Gary Gzik has been in the field of personal and professional growth for 26 years. He is an international public speaker, CEO of BizXcel Inc., a corporate trainer, a champion of Getting to Someday and an all around enthusiastic guy. Through his presentations, training seminars, audios and books, he motivates, inspires and empowers people to generate greatness through living happier and more fulfilled lives. Gary lives on the St. Lawrence River with his wife Jane, children Evan and Hannah and dogs Molly and Lilly.

ALSO BY GARY GZIK

The Orange Popsicle

In *The Orange Popsicle*, author Gary Gzik shows you how to recapture those childhood days when life was untainted by fear, boredom and routine. With compelling insights and thought-provoking anecdotes, Gzik reveals how to take the chore out of living and remove the mental blocks stopping you from embracing a life of enjoyment, happiness and fulfillment.

Page after page you will learn the vital skills necessary to turn fear into confidence, incite motivation, recapture your passion and learn the value of gratitude and the power of a positive attitude.

A book that will sweep you along, tickle your mind and stir your emotions.

Available at www.GettingToSomeday.com

KEYNOTES AND SEMINARS

When Gary Gzik steps on stage, you can't help but be drawn to his energetic, person-centered presentation style. Through personal stories, humor, and pure energy, he weaves together his experiences and his knowledge to create a dynamic presentation that passes on his passion for his own work and life to his audience. He will have any group inspired and motivated to make positive changes in all areas of their lives.

Gary began his career with the world's largest training organization and ventured into entrepreneurship in 1987. He is now CEO of BizXcel Inc., an internationally known training and consulting company, and to date has worked with over 10,000 individuals all over the world.

Gary is a versatile speaker, at home keynote speaking to 1500 people, leading a training seminar for 20 people or simply providing one-on-one management consulting. He awakens thoughts that motivate people to change the way they look at their lives and the way they do their work.

Whether at a corporate event, a not-for-profit or simply a motivational speech for a private group, Gary's rare combination of talents has given him a solid reputation with hundreds of organizations who bring him back again and again.

Gary's current programs include:

- **Putting the 'I' Back in Team**: Despite what you've been told, there IS an 'I' in team.

- **Building the Leader in You**: Put your best foot forward at work and home by taking charge of yourself first.

- **The Orange Popsicle**: Learn influential tips that will inspire you to change your life.

- **Customer Service Excellence**: Are you creating "raving fans" out of your customers?

- **Time Mastery**: One of your most valuable assets is time – are you making the most of it?

- **Increasing Resiliency**: Achieve the bounce-back personality that will keep you moving forward even in the face of challenges.

All keynotes and seminars can be customized to your specific needs.

For a full listing of Gary's courses, seminars, books, and other products, please visit the BizXcel website at **www.BizXcel.com**.

For assistance in the area of personal growth you may also wish to visit Gary's Getting to Someday site at **www.GettingToSomeday.com**. Here you will find Gary's personal growth blog, articles, and many great tips surrounding the topics in his books.

To book Gary Gzik for your next conference or event, please contact:

BizXcel Inc.
51 King Street West, Suite 201
Brockville, Ontario
Canada K6V 3P8
Phone: 613-342-2200
Fax: 613-342-2210
Email: marketing@bizxcel.com
Website: www.bizxcel.com
   www.gettingtosomeday.com

www.ingramcontent.com/pod-product-compliance
Lightning Source LLC
Chambersburg PA
CBHW051123160426
43195CB00014B/2316